Ah... memories of the Thasian sea
Sad and happy, pure and interwoven
Sometimes of the Shrove and Lenten
Sometimes of Easter... glorying in a r

Father Georgios Diamantopoulos

CONTENTS

CONTENTS

5. NORTHWESTERN THASOS

6. NORTHEASTERN THASOS

1

THASOS

The emerald island of the Aegean

Verdant green. Azure blue. Full of memories and promises. Unselfconsciously picturesque. Surprisingly unexpected. The island of Thasos surely offers one of the very few remaining opportunities to enjoy nature in an unspoiled state, to find in its simplicity the true beauty that our civilisation has repressed from its memory using the justification of its primitive nature, but chiefly owing to the fear that it has been lost for good. Dense forests of Thasos pine, black pine and Macedonian fir cover the entire surface of the island, with graphic little villages nestled among the trees waiting to be revealed to the patient visitor. Your eyes seem to be drawn like a magnet to this lush green landscape, although the slightest movement is enough to focus them on the vastness of the Aegean. Little coves, sandy beaches, steep rocks and hidden caves promise a variety of scenery and emotions. The island's white marble has been used to create some of the most beautiful sculptures in the world and its choice wine is a nectar that has intoxicated men and gods alike. The island is also famous for its honey; while wood from its forests provided timber for building many seaworthy ships. Herodotus tells of the existence of "native gold" and even if the only deposits found in the region to date are of petroleum, its wealth is undisputed.

Thasos enchants-both day and night.

With all the above, and with an even richer historical and cultural background, it is easy for Thasos to win the hearts and minds of visitors and to monopolise their conversations for a long time after they have left the island. Without any special effort and without having to resort to the science of marketing, Thasos has easily acquired a reputation that has spread to the four corners of the earth, to become a source of inspiration for writers of lovely lyrics. But the island's attractions were also the cause of its moments of great glory and great disaster, as it has always drawn colonists and conquerors from far and wide whose presence on the island frequently marked its subsequent history.

Foreign influences were quickly and constructively assimilated by the local people, who respected and kept up the customs and traditions that have accompanied the island's history over time and which lend variety to the local people's daily life as well as a picturesque note to visitors' brief stay on the island. Thasos is an earthly paradise. A true delight. A moment of creation. An opportunity to escape from our concretebound, habit-encased daily lives. Don't miss it!

Limenas.

Geography

Thasos is the northernmost island in the Aegean Sea, about 7-8 km off the coast of eastern Macedonia, not far from Keramoti and the estuary of the Nestos River. At its widest part, the island is 22 km from east to west and 26 km long from north to south. Encircled by 93 km. of coastline, it is smaller than Rhodes and larger than neighbouring Samothrace.

The highest point on the island is Ypsario, at 1127 m. above sea level, the peak of a mountain range that cuts across the island; next highest is the Profitis Ilias peak at 1108 m. The serpentine coasts of Thasos are without deep cuts or strongly projecting promontories. Starting from the northernmost point of the island and travelling eastwards, one meets the cape called Pachis or Olmanei. Here is located the little bay on which is port of Thasos or Limenas, which ends in the cape called Fourni, The Monk of Thasos or Kommeno Kavo. It is followed by the bay of Skala Panagias, which ends in the cape Gramvousa facing the islet of the same name, and across the bay is the cape of Diapyri opposite an island of the same name. Next is Cape Stavros, the bay of Themonia, which ends at the cape Demir Halkas, the bay of Kinyra, the capes of Aghios Georgios and Stavros Baboura and the southernmost cape on the island, Salonikios opposite the islet Panaghia.

From Salonikios begins the broad bay of Limenaria which ends in cape Kefalas to the southwest. On the western coast of the island, is Prinos, the second port of Thasos, located opposite the oil drilling platforms. Administratively, Thasos consists of a single municipality with its capital in Limenas and nine municipal departments. It has a population of 16,000 residents.

The two main towns (administrative and commercial) are Limenas (or Thasos) in the north of the island and Limenaria in the south. In both these towns, you will be able to find virtually all services and relatively good shopping.

The island's climate is temperate and healthy. The summer, with few exceptions, is warm and the winter not too cold. The thermometer in summer can go as high as 30-35°C, and in winter it can plunge as low as 4-8°C below zero Centigrade. But the average temperature in summer is 20-25°C and in winter 8-10°C above zero.

On Thasos, all the seasons of the year are lovely, but the most beautiful is late spring and early summer. Then the temperature is ideal and the landscape is accentuated by a thousand colours. The summer too is delightful, for the island is cooled by breezes blowing down from the mountains and off the sea. In winter, Ypsario is the first spot on the island to have snow, which contributes to creating a magic landscape with trees and snowdrops, more reminiscent of spring than winter.

THASSOS
SCALE: 1:140,000
N
Pachys
Glyfada
Thassos
(Limenas)
Palaiokastro
Glyfada
Makryammos
Agios Ioannis
Agios Georgios
Rachoni
YPSARION OROS
PROFITIS ILIAS
1127
SPATHI
Kazaviti
Panagia
Chrysi
Ammoudia
Korakia
Potamias
Potamia
Skala
Potamias
GRAMVOUSSA
GENNA
872
1204
YPSARI
Maries
Profitis Ilias
Palaiochori
VATOS
Krini
Kinyra
KINYRA
Kastro
Kinyra
Loutra
Theologos
TRIKORFON
810
Lakkos Kastrou
MANTALOUDI
TOUMPI
326
STAVRI
DIAPOROS
SAMAKERO
Thymonia
Dipotamos
Kalyves Potou
Moni
Archangelou
Alyki
Babouras
Ambas
Astris
Salonikios
LEGEND
Asphalt road
Non-Asphalt road
Minor road
Distance in km
Archaeological site
Church
Monastery
Castle
Anchorage
Beach
Cave
Camping

Flora - Fauna

Thasos has the most fertile soil of all the Aegean islands. Grains, pulses, fruit, honey, olives, oil and wine are just some of the island's products that are well known throughout Greece and making a name for themselves in the rest of the world as well.

The scrub vegetation here is unique, with its fragrant arbutus, cistus, chaste tree, myrtle, rosemary, oregano, sage and thyme. The surface of the island is mainly mountainous and rocky and is covered by dense forests of pines, oaks, firs, plane trees and horse chestnut, all trees whose timber has been used since ancient times for various purposes including ship-building. The island is full of deep gorges, little bays and velvety beaches. The combination of mountain and sea creates landscapes of rare beauty.

The major forest fires in the 1980s that destroyed a large part of the pine forest on Thasos caused large wild animals such as wolves and jackals, whose numbers had already diminished, to disappear from the island altogether. Today one can encounter foxes, hares, weasels and other smaller mammals.

The bird population is of particular interest, particularly the birds of prey, while hunters are interested in game birds such as partridge, quail and turtle doves in summer.

The Forestry Service of the Prefecture of Kavala, in its effort to protect the wildlife that remains on the island against hunters, has designated two large areas as game refuges (on Mount Ypsario and at Skala Marion) and has in fact made the hunting of hares largely illegal.

A very important element related to the animals on Thasos is the fact that the majority of sheep and goats on the island are wild (goats and sheep wander around freely in many regions, especially in mountainous areas) given that the large wild carnivores whose natural prey they would have been have disappeared.

The Thasos goat in particular is known outside of the island for its delicious meat which can even be found as far away as the meat market in Athens.

Geology

Thasos is composed of strata of metamorphic rock. These strata consist of alternating layers of gneiss, marble and schist which have been called a metamorphic system and belong geotectonically to the Rhodope zone.

Thasos rock, owing to the metamorphosis it has sustained, is difficult to describe in terms of how it came into being. The lack of fossils has hindered the task of tracing the tectonic movements that shaped the island as it is today. Most of the rock strata of Thasos however are of sedimentary origin, and have been metamorphosed over a long period of time. The oldest layers are of crystalline rock made up of the older formations of the Potamia range with layers of schist, gneiss, horizontal marble and dolomite. The names of these various rock formations have been taken from the regions in which they are found. The Potamia range occupies all the westnorthwestern part

1

of the island along the coast. It is followed by alternating veins of gneiss, marble and schist. The Maries gneiss covers a large area in the central section of the island. Marble is found on the Profitis Ilias peak The Maries gneiss contains lenticular forms of marble intrusions.

Next is a very limited area of Trikorfos marble and Kastro marble which prevails on the west, south and northwestern side of the island, virtually all along the southern and western coasts. Boubes marble is also found in limited amounts to the north and west of Kalyvia, lying above the schist of Aghios Eleftherios. The entire metamorphic system closes with the gneisses of Touba, which are found only in the south and are limited to the Touba region. More recent, non-metamorphic rock can be seen at the south-western tip of the island, west of Kalyvia and Limenaria, at cape Kefalas. This is conglomerate brecchia sandstone with thin clay overlayers from the Upper Miocene Age. The conglomerate, brecchia and argillaceous, sand and gravel deposits, which were produced mainly by the sediments deposited by streams, are believed to have been laid down about the same time and are comparatively recent.

The minerals of Thasos are smithsonites which in the past were extracted in significant quantities. Also, iron and manganese ores were found. The iron ores included limonite and hematite. Iron, copper, lead, silver and zinc mines were worked in antiquity. Today only the galleries and entranceways have been preserved. Copper-mining was also carried out in the regions of Astris, Thimonia and Kinyra. Lead and zinc can still be found at Kallirachi (Makrolakkos).

1. One part of the beautiful Thasian forests.
2. Mines at Limenaria.

2

2

MYTH & HISTORY

From the realm of myth to modern times

Mythologie

According to Greek mythology, the first settler and founder of the island was a man called Thasos who gave his name to it.

Herodotus, the famed ancient historian, reported that the island had taken the name of Thasos the Phoenician.

Thasos was either the son or grandson of Agenor, king of Phoenicia, and found himself on the island in search of Europa who had been spirited away by Zeus, who had been captivated by her. But the Phoenicians did not tolerate the rape of Europa and organised an expedition composed of many ships led by Cadmus, brother of Europa, and co-leader with Thasos, in an effort to locate her and bring her home. The search lasted for many years, and at the end the expedition separated into two. One section, led by Cadmus, went to Boeotia and built Thebes in its hinterlands; while the other section led by Thasos headed for the island of Thasos, where it settled permanently. At the same time, Europa was being sought by her other two brothers Phoenicas and Kilikas in various other places.

Broadened Thasian tetradrachm.

Another myth, which was probably shaped by the Pariansafter they settled in their new home, relates that Hercules gave Thasos to Sthenelus and Alcaeus, the sons of King Androgeus of Paros. Thus the first settler on Thasos was Thasos, from whom the island took its name.

But other than these tales, there are also other views, perhaps more valid, regarding the origin of the island's name. Some ancient poets and authors refer to Thasos by the name of "Aeria" because of its cool summer breeze, "Chrysi" because of the gold in its mines, "Edonis" derived from the Edoni Thracians and "Shore of Demeter" owing to its rich and selected variety of fruit.

According to another version, the name of Thasos is etymologically related to the word drosos (=cool) because of the many forests it had in antiquity, and continues to have today. And finally yet others associate the name of the island with weather-related words.

Fantasy IV "The Rape of Europa", 1968, woodcut by artist-engraver K. Grammatopoulos.

Inscription from the tomb of Glaucus, friend of the poet Archilochus (Archaeological Museum of Thasos).

Antiquity

The story best known to the Greeks about Thasos is the one that starts with the island's colonisation. There are, however, conflicting viewpoints as to who its first inhabitants were. One viewpoint (which is also the most widely held) argues that they were rude, warlike Thracian tribes, such as the Edoni; while according to the second view, the first inhabitants of the island were the Corians. In either case, what is certain is that Phoenician voyagers came to Thasos. They discovered and worked its mines for gold and other minerals. What is not certain is how they settled and developed a significant culture. Herodotus believed that the Phoenicians built Thasos, under the leadership of Thasos, long before the Parians appeared. According to Herodotus's version of the story (there is a second one upheld by Thucydides which will be set out below), the Phoenicians colonised Thasos, threw out the Thracians and gave themselves over to the exploiting the mines because they knew not only how to extract the ores but also how to process and sell them. Moreover, being familiar with shipbuilding and shipping, they built ships and set out on journeys to nearby coasts. At the same time, they cultivated the land and built walls around the city. While all these works were in progress, Hellenes and other tribes arrived to lend a hand; at the same time they learned about industry and crafts from the Phoenicians, and also became more familiar with their culture.

In time, the Greek element prevailed and the Phoenicians were assimilated by the Greeks who had a more dynamic numerical majority. The new colony eventually ceased to be politically dependent on Phoenicia, and its inhabitants gradually crossed over to colonise the opposite mainland shore and started working the mines on Mount Pangaeus.

According to Thucydides, the father of the scientific historiography, the first people to colonise Thasos were the Parians. Their leader was Telesikles, who undertook the mission after receiving an oracle from Delphi which said:

"Άγγειλον Παρίοις Τελεσίκλεες, ως σε κελεύω
νήσω εν Ηερίη κτίζειν ευδείελον άστω."

Translation:
Tell the Parians, Telesikles,
That I have instructed you to buld on the island Aeria
a city that will be visible from all sides."

Thus Telesikles, with the assistance of the poet Archilochus, discovered Thasos and the Thracians settled on it. According to this view, the Phoenicians did not colonise the island systematically, but worked its mines and established trading posts. Although it was difficult to expel the Thracian tribes, Telesikles managed to establish control over Thasos, and in this way was able to start building it up rapidly, and over a period of time, making it one of the most civilised and developed places in the ancient world.

It is said that it was the Parians who attacked the Thracians on the opposite shores. In their first campaign they were defeated, but in the second they were triumphant and even expelled the enemy; at the same time they found and exploited the mines on Pangaeus that had been discovered by the Phoenicians. The prevailing view in the scholarly world is the second, which has the Parians as the first colonists of the island. It was they who settled on Thasos early in the 7th century BC, an event that defines the point at which the history of Thasos essentially begins. Archaeological findings confirm their existence on the island and their eventual spread to the opposite shore. At that time (7th century BC) trading posts were established at Galepsus, Oesymi and Neapoli in the region of Mount Pangaeus.

This is also a period that produced splendid works of art. Exceptional works of metalsmith's art, pottery, miniature sculpture, sculpture and architecture have been found on and under the island's soil. Located at a crossroads of sea lanes, Thasos was open to external influences, as shown by copper and ivory artifacts which testify to relations with the Cyclades, Rhodes, Ionia, and Corinth, and in the 6th century BC, with Athens. Coins bearing representations of a satyr and nymph are widely distributed and demonstrate the extent of commercial relations as well as the periodic financial prosperity of Thasos. The town retained close ties with Paros by preserving its calendar, cults and institutions.

At the end of the archaic period, the city was so rich that it built a wall, unique for the age, of marble and schist with relief decoration on the gates and a perimeter of 4 km around the inhabited area. In 491 BC, when Darius, king of Persia and his general Mardonius invaded Thrace, the Thasians themselves were obliged to tear down the wall and become tributaries to their conquerors.

Between 480 and 478 BC, when the Persians left the Aegean, Thasos found itself once more on the side of the Hellenic city-states, embroiled in the dispute between Athens and Sparta.

In spring of 477, the Thasians were allies of Athens, and contributed 30 ships to the Delian League. It was not long before the ambitions of Cimon threatened the pre-eminence of Thasos and even of Mount Pangaeus, when Athenian colonists settled on the Nine Roads near the mouth of the Strymon river in about 465 BC. At that point the Thasians rebelled, seeking assistance and support from Sparta. Two years later, Thasos was put to a cruel siege that deprived their kings of resources, and thus, without a naval force, reduced it to the status of a subordinate city, absolutely dependent on Athens.

As time passed, the weaker Thasos became, the more Athens demanded. In 411, when the Helot revolt broke out, the local oligarchy took Thasos out of the Athens-dominated alliance. The Thasians then fortified the city and repaired their fleet but were ultimately defeated. Thus began a ten-year period during which Thasos and its prosperity were in serious jeopardy.

Early in the 4th century BC and after many disasters, Thasos tried to obliterate any sign of misunderstanding with Delphi over Neapoli with the mediation of Paros. The city acquired architectural and administrative infrastructure, the wall behind the port and inland was repaired once again, and at the same time the market (agora), the centre of civil and commercial life, was planned.

After these changes, Thasos became associated a little more closely with Paros and, after 377 BC, joined the second Delian League, in which it consolidated its influence on the mainland, while in 360 the orator Callistratus, exiled from Athens, established the town of Crinides (later Philippi) with the Thasians near Pangaeus. The fact that Thasian coins are found scattered all over the Balkan peninsula shows the economic significance of the city during the Hellenistic period. This economic power went hand in hand with some political autonomy. Late in the 3rd cent. BC, the state managed to dictate its terms to King Philip V of Macedonia who occupied the city in 202 BC.

The Hellenistic period

When Thasos joined the second Delian League in 377 BC, the Thasians used the support of Athens to extend their influence on the mainland. In 357 or 340 BC, Philip of Macedonia expanded into the area. The Thasians retained some autonomy under the kingdom of the Macedonians. In terms of city planning, the return to prosperity in the 4th and 3rd centuries BC is obvious in the relocation of the market, which then occupied the flat expanse of land between the port and first slopes of the hill, and was flanked by the great thoroughfare leading from the sanctuary of Artemis to that of Hercules.

The prosperity of the Hellenistic period has left its mark on the exhibits in the Archaeological Museum of Thasos.

Some sanctuaries were repaired and resettled (the Artemisio, the sanctuary at Evraiokastro, the Herakleio) while other new ones appeared (Posideion, Dionysion). Some new gates were built in the wall and others were repaired. During the 4th century BC, the inner wall that separated the port from the city was repaired, and the outer wall was reinforced by the addition of towers in the middle of the 3rd century BC. In the 4th century BC and in the first half of the 3rd, greater development can be seen in the constructed surface, with spacious and well organised areas and an upsurge of growth in the outlying districts. After the victory of Rome, Thasos became its loyal helper and adopted a hostile stance toward Macedonia. In 80 BC, the Thasians were rewarded by Lucius Sulla, who granted them privileges, gave the city immunity and returned to it the lands Rome had occupied on the mainland coast. Thus the status of Thasos was restored, its commerce was particularly robust and a good many wealthy Thasians began to play an active role in the political life of the region, acting as mediators between the nobles who settled in Thessaloniki and the rest of Greece. From the archaeological viewpoint, the period does not present a high level of building activity, and so the information we have from this source is minimal. In the market, the Oblique Stoa (2nd cent. BC) was built and the monument to Theogenis was erected. Generally speaking, the picture of the city then does not reflect the image that Thasos is believed to have held at that time and one has the impression that the decline which had already begun in the mid-3rd century BC intensified. The end of the Roman Republic brought significant repercussions to the island: Antony, the victor in 42 BC, imposed reprisals on Thasos because the republicans had used it as a base of operations and supplies. Even though Octavian, who would later become the emperor Augustus, eventually restored the city's privileges, its course and evolution for the next few centuries were linked to the history of Rome and its emperors, a fact which is reflected in its social life and institutions. Thasos flourished during the reign of Hadrian and continued to be prosperous until the 4th cent. AD, as shown by its sculptures and many votive offerings.

The Roman period

Thasos took advantage of the decline of Macedonia to become a devoted follower of Rome, to which it remained faithful despite the brutal seige it suffered as a consequence. But under the Romans, Thasos remained free in name only. This was why Pliny referred to it as free up to the Flavian period at which time Vespasian (69-70 AD) united Thasos with the province of Thrace; from then on, it was merely a distant province of the mighty Roman Empire. It appears, however, that while it may have forfeited its freedom during those years, it regained its former prosperity, as testified by the rich sarcophagi that have been preserved from that era. In 80 AD, it won a significant reward when Lucius Sulla forced the Senate to restore the city's privileges and immunity and to return its mainland territories.

The Thasians also played a part in the last moments of the Roman Republic. In the final confrontation at Philippi between the republicans Brutus and Cassius and their adversaries Antony and Octavian, Thasos was used, willingly or not, by the republicans as a base and provisioning centre. Cassius committed suicide after the first battle at Philippi, and Brutus had his body brought to Thasos where he was accorded final honours. There too, after the second battle and the death of Brutus, many famous Romans took refuge.

In the autumn of 42 BC, Antony, having emerged as victor, administered reprisals against the island. Fortunately this fall from favour did not last long as Augustus and his family eventually restored the city's former privileges.At the same time, its social evolution proceeded, with jobs and money in the hands of a small number of families. Women assumed priestly duties and refurbished sanctuaries at their own expense. During the years of the empire, the government in Rome tried to revitalise the aristocracy and to create a new class, the "friends of Caesar and friends of the homeland", a title conferred upon

Reproduction of Roman emperors (Archaeological Museum of Thasos).

the most distinguished Thasians, from the 1st century AD on. At the end of the 2nd cent. AD, there was a Senate among its institutions. The high priests of Augustus were engaged in buildings, bids and presentations, in order to show off their wealth. They brought in gladiators and "hunting" games and, in the middle of the second century AD, renovated the theatre.

When the province of Thrace was created during the reign of Claudius in 44 AD, Thasos benefitted by being relieved of the obligation of supplying troops and of certain chores in the mainland imperial postal service. Until the 4th century AD, Thasos remained full of vitality and prosperity. With the advent of Christianity, the number of basilicas increased, as they did at Philippi, where the Apostle Paul gave his first sermon on European soil. And finally, during the Byzantine period, Thasos became the seat of a bishopric.

The Byzantine period

The beginning of the Byzantine era coincided with the end of the Thasian state and culture. The information provided to us by Byzantine chroniclers about Thasos at that time is sparse, confused, and incomplete. The Christian religion was made known on the island in 52 AD when St Paul travelled from Troy (in present day Asia Minor) to Neapoli (now Kavala). Christianity spread rapidly, but the the fact was slow to manifest itself because the authorities on the island took great pains not to displease Rome, whose religion was pagan and whose stance toward Christianity hostile. During the early Byzantine years, Thasos prospered and its inhabitants built beautiful churches.

The sixth century was when the raids began. Invaders of the island would sweep down from north, east and west. First it was the Avars who first seized Thasos, during the reign of Justinian. In 765, Slav pirates captured the island and put the majority of its inhabitants to flight. The Byzantine emperor Constantine Copronymus, known for his involvement in the Iconomachy, was unable to recapture the island and had to enter into negotiations with the pirates. In 904, the Saracens arrived in Thasos fresh from their occupation of Crete. They built ships and seige engines. At the same time, they plundered the island and transported many of its inhabitants to Candia in Crete (today's Herakleion) where they were sold as slaves. In 961, Thasos was once again incorporated into the Byzantine state, and made part of the theme of Thrace, which it remained until 1204 when Constantinople was sacked by the Crusaders. In that same year, Thasos was given to the Enrico Dandolo, doge of Venice. The Venetians built a palace on the acropolis, repaired the wall according to the specifications of the age, and constructed large towers at various points in the city, the ruins of which can be seen to this day.

Thasos returned once again to the Byzantine state in 1261, when Constantinople was recaptured by Michael Palaeologus. In 1306, the island was oppressed by Tidedias Zacharias; a few years later it was sacked by the Knights of St John, and then by the Venetians, Spaniards and other raiders. In 1315, Andronicus II tried to take the island away from the Catalans, but his effort resulted in failure. The Byzantine Empire fell in 1453, but Thasos remained in the hands of the Gateluzzi family until it was taken over by the Turks.

Frankish and Venetian rule

When Constantinople was sacked by the Latins in 1204, Thasos was given to Enrico Dandolo, blind doge of Venice (1204). From then on, a number of other potential conquerors cast an envious eye on the beautiful island. In 1306, the Byzantine emperor Michael Palaeologus, having recaptured Constantinople, gave Thasos to the Genoese adventurer Francisco Gateluzzi. At that time Thasos developed greatly, mainly in the realm of trade. The Gateluzzi family remained on the island until 1455 AD, when Thasos fell into the hands of the Ottoman Turks. In 1457, Pope Callistus III sent 16 ships to the Greek seas to liberate the Christians.

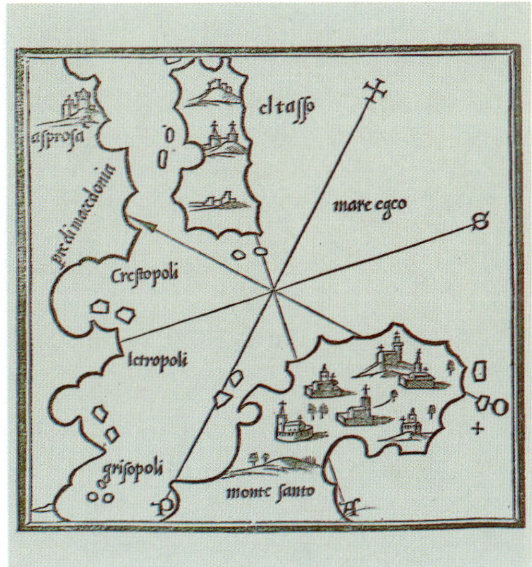

Map of Thasos, woodcut by Benedetto Badone, Gennadios Library, 1538.

Example of a Byzantine church.

The Thasians revolted and helped the Venetians capture the island. But the Turks were victorious, and the Thasians were made to suffer terribly as a result. Nevertheless during the century that followed, all events seem to have unfolded in an atmosphere of calm. At the end of the 17th century, the pirates returned, this time more vigorously. Sicilians, Venetians, Genoese, Slavs, Catalans, Spaniards and even Greek pirates invaded cities and towns, destroying and plundering the efforts of years.

Period of Turkish rule

Thasos was taken by the Turks in 1455, two years after the fall of Constantinople, when Mahmud II organised his campaign against the peninsula of Aenos, and simultaneously sent ten ships to Thasos, Samothrace and Imvros. This event led Pope Callistus III to appeal for a crusade to be launched in order to take back the islands that had fallen into the hands of the Sultan. So the crusade ships arrived at Thasos in 1457 and the Venetians managed after a brief seige to capture the island. But the fleet of the Latins was not sufficient to keep the Sultan at bay and he recaptured Thasos and Samothrace in October of 1459, under the leadership of Captain Pasha Zagan.

This event proved devastating to Thasos because at the same time, under orders from Mahmud II, most of the island's inhabitants were banished to Constantinople with the result that the island remained completely bereft of human habitation for a while. In the following year, it was granted to Demetrius Palaeologus, as a "reward" for some treachery on his part, but by the end of the summer of 1466, Thasos, together with Samothrace and Imvros, was taken by the Venetian admiral Capelo. Thasos was to experience even greater sufferings around the turn of the 18th century when piracy once again flourished in the Aegean. To protect themselves, the inhabitants abandoned the coasts and moved their villages to the mountainous hinterland, to regions protected by nature. Only the viglaria, the ancient guardposts, remained on the coast as sentinels to send warnings of danger to those inland. It is worth noting that the pirates were pure-blooded Europeans, even Greeks, whose ruthlessness was greater than that of the Saracens. They believed that their profession was honest and dignified and taught it to their children. They maintained relations and correspondence with highly placed persons and with kings, whose holidays they often helped organise, for the right price on both sides, of course.

At the same time, one more misfortune came to strike the already sorely tried inhabitants of the island. In 1760 Thasos was leased to the Master of the Horse, and its inhabitants were obliged to pay a poll tax and various other taxes into the hands of the elder of the Greek community (kotsabasis), who oppressed and tyrannized his compatriots. The Greek uprising in 1770 found the Thasians prepared to revolt. The cause was the victory of the Russian fleet against Capudan Pasha at Cesme. This led a Thasian delegation to meet with representatives from the other islands to congratulate the victors all together. In the summer of the same year, a squadron from the Russian fleet sailed to Thasos to protect its timber for ship building. Four years later the Russians withdrew and Thasos once again fell under Turkish sovereignty. Then, the Sultan's rule became even more oppressive. By the end of the 18th century, as a result of all these vicissitudes, no more than 2500 inhabitants remained on the island, and they lived in constant fear of pirates.

Egyptian rule

In 1813, the Sultan ceded Thasos to the viceroy of Egypt, Muhammad Ali, as a reward. The viceroy, later pasha, was well disposed toward the Thasians because of the fact that he had been born in Kavala and grew up in a village on the island with a Greek family. So he allowed a special regime to be established on the island with some degree of community self-government that lasted until 1874.

Specifically, each community was headed by the president of the elders, the so-called tsorbatzis, *who assumed responsibilities in respect of the Egyptian authorities to whom he was accountable. The presidents from all the villages would gather together to elect the* bachtsorbatzis, *i.e. the president of the entire island.*

Modern history

Around the time of the Greek War of Independence in 1821, Thasos was experiencing a brief interlude of freedom, when Greek revolutionaries sailed to the island and the tsorbatzis became the leader of the revolutionary movement.

At that time, the Turks were defeated, and withdrew to Kavala. But this state did not last long, because fear of pirates led the Thasians to seek help from the Pasha of Thessaloniki. Late in 1821, they signed a treaty with him, an action which enraged the seamen from Psara because it caused their uprising to fail.

As the Greek War of Independence progressed, Thasos and the other islands raised the flag of the revolution, in punishment for which more than 1000 people were butchered, others were put to torture and many lost their property. A few years before the Greek revolution, the Sultan of the Ottoman Empire Mahmut II, in recognition of the services that had been rendered to him by Muhammad Ali, founder of the dynasty that was to rule Egypt from the early 19th to the mid-20th century, gave him Thasos as a gift in 1814.

Muhammad made Thasos a privileged island and made its inhabitants autonomous. The Young Turks, however, after the proclamation of the new Turkish constitution and when the kedhive in Egypt was Abbas Hilmi Pasha, abolished all the privileges that the inhabitants of the island had enjoyed since the time of Muhammad Ali. Thasos remained under the administration of of Abbas Hilmi until the Balkan Wars, when it was liberated by the Greek army and fleet (8 October 1912). Since then Thasos has been part of the Hellenic Republic, as set out in the Treaty of Bucharest. The Turks regained Thasos in 1902 and up to 1912 it was under their sovereignty. During the entire period, teachers, priests and scholars cultivated a Greek national consciousness. Thus September 1912 found the Greeks patriotically, psychologically and mentally prepared to fight, alongside the Bulgarians and the Serbs, in order to eliminate the Ottoman yoke from the islands and the regions around Mount Olympus. In June 1912, the Bulgarians attacked the Serbs at Yevyeli and the Greeks in the liberated regions, an event that signalled the outbreak of the Second Balkan War. Then action began by the Greek fleet in the Aegean which led in October 1912 to the signing of the decree by Admiral Koundouriotis. On the 18th of the same month, the "Lonchi" and "Thyella", antitorpedo boats of the fleet, accompanied by the troopship "Pelos", captured Thasos. After the island was liberated, Constantinos Melas, brother of the famous Macedonian fighter Pavlos Melas, was appointed temporary administrator. In a letter to Penelope Delta, he remarked that Thasos was the most beautiful of all Greek islands: "A paradise with genuine Greeks, unwavering patriots and sensitive people".

The most significant events that took place on the island in the period between the world wars were the arrival of the refugees from Asia Minor and Thrace after the disaster in 1922, and the expropriation, on the initiative of the MP Augustus Theologitis, of property belonging to Mount Athos monasteries, which was then distributed to the island's inhabitants.

Today, the island of Thasos is an idyllic tourist spot. Hotels and roads have been built and good transportation is provided by ship and hydrofoil. All this has contributed to the financial development of the island. Gradually, Thasos has begun to regain its old glamour and once again to be recognisable as the lovely paradise described by Constantine Melas, and so many other authors, poets and travellers, from Greece and abroad.

3

CULTURE & TRADITION

Customs & manners - Cultural events
People & occupations - Arts & letters

Traditional dress.

Perhaps Cavafy was right. It's the voyage that matters. Not the destination, and even less the setting out. But some destinations may be different, such as those that cast doubt upon even the need for change which is so much a part of human frailty. The island of Thasos has everything necessary to offer a different sort of voyage. This is mainly because its beauty is unexploited, natural, authentic, capable of creating a correspondingly genuine culture. Its people exude generous feelings and restore the faith of any remaining dreamers in the authenticity of human relations. On Thasos, tourism is seen as hospitality rather than as an end in itself. The people are unaffected and genial; they are also distinguished by the respect with which they treat the traditions, customs and manners of their island.

They know that these traditions represent a source of strength that has joined them together frequently in the past, uniting them against common enemies. Religious feeling, another characteristic expression of culture, is likewise strong here and related directly with the memories of the past when the human will by itself did not seem to be enough. Arts and letters achieved a creative blend of the local people's habits and way of life with input from the invaders who conquered the island from time to time. Thasian architecture features spare structures of wood and stone in absolute harmony with the natural environment and with the character of the people.

Generally speaking Thasos gives us an opportunity to become acquainted with a different culture, one which will lend meaning to all of our destinations.

Boatyard in Limenas.

Customs & Manners

A place's customs and manners bear witness to the deeper concerns of its people as imprinted on their behaviour over a long period of time. The inhabitants of the island of Thasos know how to respect their traditions, since their entire history, with all their struggles and concerns can be traced through these traditions. The customs of Thasos express wishes that frequently give rise to the celebration of special feasts and festivities.

The need for social communication, but also the desire for an auspicious future have in some way shaped the New Year's customs. *A wide variety of food is cooked in preparation for the great feast, and customs that indicate concern for the coming year are observed. Among the best known customs are the* carols (kalanta), *which are songs of praise and good wishes, usually sung by children from door to door on the eve of the New Year. In each house they visit, they will be asked to sing in front of the icon or at some other point in the house, and at the end they are given some "good things"* (kaloudia), *i.e. money, walnuts, dried figs or roses.*

The rest of the day is spent preparing food and sweets *to be consumed the next day. The New Year's Day table must be laden with abundant food as an omen to ensure that the entire new year will be equally as rich in good things. The table is laid with great care and all the food items placed on it symbolise wishes for the new year. Honey represents the wish that the year be sweet, the fruit and olive branches express the hope that the coming year will be characterised by happiness, strength and growth, etc. Starting in the morning of New Year's Eve, every housewife prepares the St Basil's pie* (vasilopitta) *a large round loaf of sweetbread with a coin* (paras) *in it. The coin, a small token amount, is placed inside the pie to bring joy and prosperity to whoever finds it in their piece. Before putting the pie in the oven, the housewife usually takes two large forks with which she "draws" either a large cross, or the digits of the new year on the top of the pie. The pie is cut that same evening, after it has been blessed in the sign of the cross with a burning censer, and everybody has sung the hymn "εις πάσαν γην εξήλθεν".*

Then the man of the house, with a large knife, makes the sign of the cross over the pie and cuts it. The first piece is set aside for St. Basil, the second for Christ and the Virgin, and the third for the house; then pieces are cut for all family members, for the oxen used in ploughing, and for the caique (if there is one).

Another custom of the day is the spordisma *of the leaves which takes place as follows: everybody is seated around the lighted hearth; each one pulls glowing embers out of the fire and tosses an olive leaf on top of them with a wish in mind, which has not been told to anyone else. The person whose leaf twists most will have his or her wish come true.*

After all the preparations have been made, the housewife must get up at dawn on New Year's Day, bring in a heavy stone from outside, stand with it in the entrance to the house, and wake everybody in the house up with good wishes that she repeats three times: "oula kakar-kakar ki enas koukour-koukour", which roughly translated means "all are young hens with just one rooster". If nothing else, this phrase recognises the patriarchal structure of the family.

When the year changes, the custom of the podariko *is also observed, according to which, the first person to step into the house must be regarded as a lucky person and consequently capable of bringing luck and prosperity to the house. For this reason, the task of being the first person to cross the threshold is usually assigned to a child, since children are commonly believed to be the purest most innocent harbingers of happiness. Whoever enters the house first brings along a rock that is carried in and out three times with the wish "may the housewife's bag weigh as much as this stone".*

When all the family members are up, after the podariko, they go to church. Usually the grandmother of the house takes a pomegranate with her to be blessed. When the family return home, they break open the pomegranate in front of the door, so that success will disperse in the house like the red seeds of the pomegranate and fill it as the fruit is full of seeds.

Others lay the table, and the head of the house, when breaking the pomegranate exclaims: *"As the pomegranate breaks, let all our enemies be broken"*.

The pre-Lenten **carnival** is a feast with deep roots. Its culmination is on Clean Monday, the first day of Lent. All during the week before Clean Monday, young and old alike dress up in costumes made of whatever they can find at that moment, as long as they cannot be recognised. Every evening parties of people dance round their villages singing various "provocative" carnival songs. They visit friends' houses or coffee shops. At the same time, preparations begin for the fantastic event with which the celebrations culminate. Floats are made for the parade on Clean Monday, and "specialists" write poems and speeches which the masqueraders will recite. Preparations are completed on Sunday, and that evening the great feast begins. Two or three people dressed in carnival clothes make the rounds of the coffee shops reciting the ribald poems they have written themselves.

One of the most characteristic and entertaining customs at carnival time is the the **grinding of the pepper**, a custom that started out from the village of Panaghia. It lends a special delight to the party that ends at dawn on Clean Monday. It's a kind of game. One of the revellers, holding a belt or broomstick to hit infringers, is the leader. He sings a song once which the others repeat as they dance. The people who are dancing in the style of a hasaposerviko (fast folk dance by women and men holding each other by the shoulders and dancing in a circle), must follow what the leader sings with the appropriate movements. The leader punishes infringers, i.e. anyone who doesn't follow his dictates correctly, by whacking them lightly.

When this custom is finished, the party continues until dawn on Monday, when the purely formal part of the event begins. Housewives place on their balconies anything of a folk nature for the visitors to admire. Many floats join the parade; their themes are usually taken from current events or from mythology, such as Paris's Abduction of Helen, the Trojan War, the Wooden Horse, and many others.

Group of masquerades at the Thasos carnival.

Obviously all these classical themes are treated in a satirical spirit. On every street corner, there are improvised stands where wine is handed out to quench the visitors' thirst. Along all the streets and lanes, singing can be heard, most people have blackened their faces and are doing funny improvised dances. Others, wearing animal skins and large bells keep everybody in peals of laughter with their antics. Violins, lutes, and drums of the types used in past centuries, as well as instruments from Asia Minor, play cheery tunes, arousing young and old alike.

Another well known custom, that is honoured faithfully every year on the second day after Easter in the town of Kalyvia Limenaria, is called "Gia vrex Aprili mou", (Rain, my good April). It is a spring event about which tradition says that the residents of the island gathered together and prayed to God for rain so that their vines would not dry out and that they would be sure to have good crops of grapes and sweet Thasian wine. At this event, appetizers, traditional sweets and abundant wine are passed around.

Weddings: *Marriage and the customs associated with it could not but hold an very important place in the cultural development of Thasos, since a wedding was undoubtedly a significant social event. According to the traditions of Thasos, the most virtuous and socially acceptable version of marriage was when it started out correctly, exclusively through the matchmaking process. There is even a song that talks about these instances. Roughly translated it means:*

"If you love me, young man
why do you keep passing by without ever speaking;
Send matchmakers to my mother
and arrangers of marriage to my uncle."

Matchmaking was in fact nothing more than a process of intercession, the purpose of which was to introduce two young people with a view to marriage. As can be easily understood, whether or not the young candidate bride and groom were in love was not regarded as a necessary condition. The matchmaker who would undertake to establish the acquaintanceship or a proposal of marriage had to be a respected person, either a friend or relative of the family, or a trusted elderly lady. The proposal could either be made by the bride's family to that of the groom or vice versa.

The matchmaker would bring a small gift or sweets as "signs" from one family to the other. The main requirements for the matchmaking to begin would be the age of the candidates, i.e. the groom had to be over 18 years old and the bride over 15. The financial status and occupation of the groom, or the dowry and property of the girl were taken into account in the decision-making process. In addition, the moral standing, character and reputation of both, and the family name of the person making the match in the village community constituted other factors to be considered. The "word" i.e. the promise of marriage, was usually given on a Sunday.

After the match was arranged and the financial considerations sorted out, the last preparations for the wedding began a week beforehand, for most of which the bride's family were responsible. Her friends started washing the various items in her dowry - linens, embroidery etc. - on the Monday.

On Wednesday, they all sang as they ironed everything, and then folded it carefully and put it in large baskets, taking care that the corners of the white embroidery were visible hanging down at the sides. On Friday, people visited the bride's home. They examined the dowry, gave the bride silver for luck, counted the items in the dowry, to provide grist for the gossip mill later, and were given treats to eat. At a specified time, which was determined in advance, the groom would arrive with the best man, to the accompaniment of lutes and violins, and take the dowry. The mules used to transport it were decorated with kerchiefs attached to the reins. On each mule, a boy would be seated and then the procession would start out, headed by the musicians. As soon as the procession arrived at the groom's house, his mother would in turn inspect the dowry and have it unloaded in the courtyard of the house. After everybody had danced around it, they put it all in the house. On the wedding day, before the bride's friends began to dress her, her mother took her aside in a room by themselves to pass on the last pieces of advice. She would tie a little lock around her daughter's waist, lock it and put a net over it to protect her against the evil eye and magic spells. When the time came for the best man and the groom to come and pick up the bride, her friends closed her in her room and called out from inside: "Promise us something, o groom, so we give her to you".

The groom usually promised the girls a party, but sometimes, if he were a very strong-minded young man, he would ignore them and break down the door to get the bride. After the ceremony, the young couple were given money, gold sovereigns, coins and jewellery which would be pinned to the groom's lapel. As soon as they arrived at their home, the bride would go up the stairs, kneel before her mother-in-law, and kiss her hand; then the latter would give the couple a sweet from the same spoon and thus symbolically, but officially, their life together began. For anyone who has not been lucky enough to attend a real Thasian wedding, in mid-summer in the village of Theologos, which is the old capital of the island, events are held in honour of the Thasian wedding. This is in essence a traditional ceremony representing a wedding and attracts the attention of many people including tourists who may be visiting the island at that time.

Childbirth *was handled in a similarly social way in Thasos. The woman who was about to give birth was called "katavari" (very heavy), because she was burdened with the weight of the unborn child and had the respect of all, both in the immediate family and in the broader social sphere in which she lived. The pregnant woman did not go to funerals, nor did she ever see a dead person, because it was considered to bring bad luck. On her hearth, logs were never placed with the thick side down, so that the baby wasn't born "upside down". More generally, the expectant mother had to deal not only with the physical weight of the pregnancy but also with the emotional weight of the superstititions created by human ignorance in such circumstances.*

By having a good time, the residents of Thasos pay homage to their traditions and to the joys of life.

It is worth mentioning the refined taste of the inhabitants of Thasos, which is reflected in the island's **local dress**, *an essential part of every major feast. Bridal fabrics in particular were of fine silk or of cotton and silk. The best of these were adorned at the breast and around the sleeves with silk needle-lace trimming. On top they wore the* alatza, *a vest with narrow sleeves ending in "tongues", or pointed extensions of the sleeves, made of striped silk or silk and cotton by a tailor on the island, with gold embroidery by the same person at the bosom and on the tongues. Brides also wore a sleeveless dress, again tailor-made of expensive material or taffeta, embroidered in gold on the bodice. At the waist, brides wore a silk apron decorated with frills all around, with lace of gold or other colours. The belt was decorated with enamel, very similar in type to the Thracian belts. Of all the bride's wedding garments, the black felt vest was the most heavily embroidered in gold, and for this reason,*

the tailor and embroiderer were paid in gold sovereigns. Early this century, the sleeve points were added to the felt vest, thus making it appear to have double sleeves. The shirt was closed at the breast with a pin made of gold and sometimes diamonds. Thasian women's hair was usually braided. The braids were wrapped around a small red cap the domed top of which was embroidered in gold with 4 or 5 coins attached. Either under or over the braids, a yellow printed cotton kerchief was wound. And finally, for everyday wear or for going to church, women wore a woollen shawl with printed decoration around their shoulders. Stockings, knitted or bought were white, wool in winter and cotton in summer. Velvet embroidered slippers were the initial customary footwear of Thasian women, but they were rapidly replaced by laced black leather shoes. One can see traditional Thasian dress at various cultural events on the island in which folk dancing groups (phot. 1) take part and at the Municipal Museum in Kavala (photo. 2).

1

2

People & occupations

A beautiful island like Thasos, with its verdant natural environment, could not fail to have produced people of a character commensurate with this beauty. Its inhabitants are distinguished by their unaffected charm; they adapt to the island's pace of life which is serene and langorous in winter and more intense under the summer sun. Thasians have learned how to adjust to change and to accept it in good spirits. They are hospitable, warm-hearted and fun-loving, and you may be sure that they will be delighted to answer any questions you may have during your stay on their island. The people of Thasos are also deeply religious, observing their religious traditions conscientiously, a fact which can easily be demonstrated by the number of churches on the island. Hard working and restless, Thasians have sailed the seas all over the world and in the process have developed into excellent seamen. Even those who were charmed by the sea but never left home managed to make the best possible use of their land. You will not fail to be moved by the smile of the Thasians and their zest for life.

The sea sculpts people,
it shapes their customs and occupations.

The main occupations of the inhabitants of Thasos have always been related to the sea, and now more recently, to tourism. Thus it is hardly strange that until the late 19th, early 20th century, the inhabitants of the island were primarily employed as **seamen**. *The ports they visited most were Istanbul, Hydra, Thessaloniki, Piraeus, and then the smaller ports of Kavala, Keramoti, Porto Lagos, Alexandroupoli, Volos, Limnos, and Mytilini.*

They would often sail as far as the Black Sea, Romania, Russia, Egypt and Italy. The life of a seafarer then was a tough one, requiring a great deal of experience, nautical skill, courage and daring. Uneducated people without compasses, machines, maps or weather reports managed to sail the seas and are to this day considered to be among the most celebrated sailors and merchants.

The growth of tourism on the island is an enterprise to which the inhabitants of Thasos have devoted more and more of their efforts in recent years, endeavouring to ensure quality, and not just temporary commercial profit. People like the Thasians, who love traditions and keep them up, have also made sure to preserve some of the old-time crafts. For this reason, apart from the sea and tourism, which are their basic occupations, women and men alike continue to practise skills and crafts that have been handed down for generations.

The people of Thasos made their living from the occupations of seafarer or shipbuilder for many years.

Folk weaving, *in comparison to shop weaving, is a household craft, i.e. done at home. This type of weaving must be considered an art because the weaver is not engaged in the mass reproduction of motifs, but creates her own, reshaping, adding, subtracting and improving. This is how she keeps the tradition alive. Examples of folk weaving can be dated mainly from the 18th century. The beauty of the designs, in conjunction with the vivid colours lend this type of weaving an even greater value. The wonderful motifs and quality of the textiles are admired by local people and tourists alike. Moreover, folk weaving serves the needs of the inhabitants, not only by bringing in revenues, but by its function as a way of life, a solution to problems, a link with the history of the island and a strong bond with nature.*

Folk weaving is a true art on Thasos.

Pottery is another favourite occupation of the Thasians. The first permanent pottery workshop on the island was set up in 1910 at Limenas; its output combined elements from northern mainland and Cycladic art. In 1935, this workshop split up into two separate producers of ceramic ware. In one, large outdoor settling tanks on several levels were used, and then there were special areas for drying, a foot-operated wheel and a wood-burning kiln. The current output covers the needs of the tourist market; it is worth noting here that modern pottery production has been influenced by the style of Sifnos, in terms of both shapes and colours.

The lush olive groves *and* beehives *on Thasos also require dedication from its inhabitants. The island has been famous from ancient times up to the present for its production of olives and olive oil. The entire island is dotted with olive groves spreading out like a silver-green carpet on the hillsides beside the sea. The season when the olives are gathered is a real festival. Everyone, old and young lends a hand, starting early in the morning and ending at dusk.*

The unique quality of Thasian olives is known throughout Greece and beyond. Its oil, clear and golden coloured, is healthy, flavourful and much in demand in all the surrounding areas.

In equal demand is Thasian honey from the hives that can be seen in the most beautiful spots on the island, standing among the lush forests and flower-strewn meadows.
Honey and royal jelly are among the island's most sought-after products. Many families keep bees, because apart from the obvious commercial reasons, in this way they also ensure a regular supply of honey for their family.

It could be said generally that the rich soil of Thasos caused the Thasians to develop trade to enable them to transport the oil, honey, wine and whatever else their island produced, to other parts of Greece.

Pottery and the production of oil from the island's splendid olive groves are among the Thasians' most frequent occupations.

Another pastime on Thasos is the preparation of delicious traditional food from the **local cuisine.**

The women of Thasos are proud of the local foods they prepare and are, by tradition, celebrated for their culinary skills, while Thasian sweets have gained a reputation beyond the borders of Greece. It is obvious that one can find fresh fish on Thasos, but the wise visitor will know enough to ask for "liokafto" and "skoubri sona" which is fish cut and open down the middle and charcoal grilled. "Liasto ktapodaki" or sun-dried octapus is the best appetizer to accompany Thasian ouzo or a similar beverage called tsipouro.

Thasos is famous for its roast goat, especially at Theologos where it is a specialty, since in the mountainous parts of the island there are still wild goats and other wild creatures whose meat is particularly tasty. A traditional vegetable dish is called paterika, *which consists of large cabbage leaves cooked with tomatoes, olive oil and onions. The olives of Thasos, a major export item, are famous as* throumbes *(with savoury) and rarely absent from the Thasian table.*

Thasian sweets are so well known that there is an entire cottage industry today that prepares and markets them. Among the best known are walnut spoon sweets (karydaki) *and Thasian halvas. Food is always accompanied by the island's traditional red wine.*

The inhabitants of Thasos are an inventive and clever people; they love their homeland and leave it only with great difficulty. But even when they are obliged to depart from their island, all their thoughts and their purpose in life is directed toward returning. The same is true of visitors; those who have been lucky enough to visit Thasos look forward to returning at the first opportunity; for they find it hard to relinquish the memories of this lovely island.

Thasian honey is famous, and the local cuisine is rich in marine delicacies.

Arts & letters

The island of Thasos has a significant artistic and cultural heritage, which has distinguished the island since ancient times. Moreover, the passage of so many visitors could not but further enrich the already remarkable cultural heritage of Thasos and influence her talented artists.

With respect to the **arts***, one of the best known Thasian artists in antiquity, and a pioneer of Hellenic painting, was the painter and sculptor* **Polygnotus***. His creations were so admired that when Cimon captured Thasos, he persuaded Polygnotus to follow him to Athens. From then on, the Thasian's incomparable talent became widely known all over Hellas. Polygnotus decorated the walls of the Poikile Stoa, the Theseion and the Anakeion with his paintings and murals, and two of his paintings were discovered in the Propylaea. Because he would not accept remuneration for all these paintings, the Athenians bestowed upon him the honour of Athenian citizenship.*

Paintings by Polygnotus could also be seen at Plataea, in the temple of Areia Athena and in the hall of the Cnidians at Delphi. His works were inspired by the Homeric epics and by myths, legends and traditions. A characteristic of his art was the beauty of his drawing, his composition and his "ethos" or characterisation. He is regarded by many as having been the greatest painter of antiquity. He is also reputed to have created sculptures.

Other ancient Thasian artists were the artist Aglaophon, father of Polygnotus, who gave the latter his first drawing lessons. **Aristophon***, brother of Polygnotus, was also a painter. Among his best known works was the depiction of Philoctetes in pain.* **Aglaophon***, another painter from the same family, and nephew of Polygnotus, was commissioned by Alcibiades to paint two works.* **Sosikles***, a sculptor, won third prize in a contest at Ephesus where he had submitted a work depicting a wounded Amazon. In the same contest, the first and second prize went to Polygnotus and Pheidias respectively.*

One of the most significant sculptors of antiquity was **Pythagoras** *of Rhegium, to whom is attributed the statue of the Thasian athlete Theogenis.*

In modern times, the artist who stands out and has paid homage to Thasos in his works and actions, is the sculptor Polygnotus Vaghis, a multi-talented and highly productive creator. Almost 25 centuries separate him from the ancient Polygnotus, but their fame is as great and their works equally admired.

Polygnotus Vaghis *was born in Potamia in 1894 and at the age of 16 left for the U.S. where he studied at the School of Fine Arts in Washington DC. A tireless worker, he became one of the top sculptors of the period. His works are exhibited today in some of the finest museums and art galleries in America and in just a few private collections, because he wanted them to be accessible to the public. Polygnotus Vaghis died in the U.S. in April of 1965 having bequeathed all his remaining works of art to the Greek state. Greece awarded him the Phoenix medal.*

In the field of **letters** *too, Thasos has a rich heritage.* **Hegemon***, who was born in Thasos, is regarded as having invented the parody. He was in addition an excellent writer of comedies, a poet and an actor. He moved to Athens during the Peloponnesian War where he became famous as a writer of comedies; unfortunately however, none of them are extant.*

Stesimbrotus*, a contemporary of Cimon and Pericles, was a sophist and orator. Even though he too was born and brought up in Thasos, he left for Athens where he was highly paid to teach the Homeric epics. He was said to have written a political pamphlet on Themistocles, Thucydides and Pericles, and books about the mysteries and about Homer. His efforts met the same fate as the work of the other sophists.*

And finally, **Androsthenis***, who accompanied Alexander the Great on his campaign against Asia, recorded his impressions in a work entitled "Wanderings in India".*

Architecture

The architecture of the houses in Thasos bears no resemblance to that of the other Aegean islands. Perhaps because this island is completely different from the other islands in the region. During the period when communication between the island and the mainland towns of Keramoti and Kavala was very difficult, the material available for building houses in Thasos was only rock and wood, materials which could be found in abundance on the island. This is why the traditional Thasian house is so much a part of its natural environment. Although the majority of craftsmen were local people, there were many Epirot and Bulgarian artisans working there at the same time.

Traditional houses *on the island of Thasos were built parallel to the slope of the ground, which is usually steep, rather than vertical to it. Most times, there was a rectangular or square facade; mansions usually had more complex facades.*

Also, because of the slope of the terrain, the houses are two-storeyed, rarely three-storeyed. The ground floor, called the katoi *of the house, functions as a storage area for oil, olives, wine and the other commodities, or as a stable for the animals. This part of the house is usually built of stone and timber. It could be one single space or built in two sections with a stone wall in between. The area is lighted by loophole-like openings. Sometimes, apart from storage areas, there might also be a room. The* katoi *is linked with the floor above by wood or stone stairs. The wall in the middle of the basement extends to the upper floor as far as the roof which it supports. The interior walls of the upper floor are made of* tsatmas, *the local term for brick covered with thin boards and a mixture of lime and straw. The most official room of the house, which is used to receive visitors is the* ondas. *It does not have a fireplace, but has many windows and a beamed wooden ceiling or central cupola. The other areas of the house are the bedrooms. These rooms, either with*

Houses on Thasos are constructed of stone and wood.

or without ceilings have a fireplace and niches or windows, right and left. The house has no kitchen. The kitchen appeared much later, and the area it occupied was relatively small. The washrooms are almost always outside.

The Thasian house was sparsely furnished. Its most important pieces of furniture were the sofras *(a low round table for serving food), wooden sofas, mattresses and later wooden bed frames and stools. The floor was covered by Thasian rugs, woven on the loom, while the walls were hung with kilims of characteristic geometric design. The exterior of the house's upper floor was usually built of stone. In the beginning, the facades of the houses were all equipped with a* hagiati*, i.e. a roofed veranda which was open on one or two sides, and which had one or two rooms behind it that would be lighted through the hagiati. Of course not all the houses on Thasos had hagiatia. As time passed, these walls were closed and stairs were created. Houses with a sitting room may have triangular projections parallel to the facade or small wooden balconies. Houses with similar features can also be found in Halkidiki. Variations on the sitting room can be found in the village of Panaghia, where the area is open on two sides.*

There is also another type of house on the island called **adelphomoiria***, houses which have been divided into two equal sections on both the ground floor and the upper floor, and were designed to house two grown children and their respective families. The roof of the houses is wooden and is always covered by slate tiles. The windows have two panels and for greater security, some of them are reinforced by horizontal iron bars. The outer doors are wooden, studded at the lower level, with two panels, a large opening and an arched lintel. All are secured with a wooden bar. The inner doors are more richly decorated. Today just a few of these traditional Thasian houses remain. But those that have been preserved are truly remarkable.*

Four views of traditional architecture.

4 THE TOWN & THE

The town of Thasos or Limenas has been the island's most important town since ancient times. It is the capital, venue for almost everything happening on the island. Yesterday's town and today's town. The ancient town which awakens memories of another age and the modern town which is steadily developing into a tourist centre of international stature. It isn't hard to read the signs from the different historical periods. The ancient city reflects the fear of invasion, a defensive mood and a feeling of insecurity, reflecting the instability created by the periodic invasions to which the island has was subjected.

ANCIENT SITES OF LIMENAS

Its modern successor radiates the aura of security and renewal of a town enjoying continuing progress and prosperity.

The atmosphere of the ancient city recalls the wisdom of antiquity and, through it, the wisdom of all the island's subsequent invaders. The modern town was constructed out of the longing of a whole generation of refugees to recover their lost homeland. The ancient city is mysterious. The modern town is itself a mystery. The mystery of evolution and of the power of history. The town itself is the same.

The **ancient city** was built on the same site as the present-day capital Limenas, the other name for the town of Thasos, which extends over two neighbouring hills as far as the wall, and down into a small section of the surrounding plain. Around it there was a high, impregnable wall constructed of huge rectantular marble blocks and slabs of slate. It was in the form of an irregular polygon with a perimeter of about four kilometres. The ancient wall had been built by the first settlers, Phoenicians or Parians. It was later reinforced to provide better protection from invaders but included numerous gates enabling the inhabitants to communicate freely with the surrounding countryside. Some of these gates have been preserved to the present day and on them one can see remarkable bas-reliefs depicting gods and heroes, as well as inscriptions and dedications.

The highest point of the city was the Acropolis or citadel, which was surrounded by a high wall. It was here that the wealth of the entire state was kept, including the public treasury; it was also designed as a defence bastion of last resort, in the event that invaders should succeed in breaching the city wall. At some time during the Middle Ages the citadel was repaired, chiefly by the Venetians and Genoans, at which time it sustained numerous alterations. Two towers, a water cistern and a ruined chapel survive today on the Acropolis.

The city had two harbours: the military port, which survives and is still in use to this day, and the commercial one, which used to be alongside it but has unfortunately been destroyed. All that remains of it is a section of its foundations, which are under the sea and can be viewed from the high ground opposite.

Both harbours were outside the wall, which was interrupted at that point but continued some distance further on. Its purpose was to protect the town in the event of invaders capturing the harbours. There were impressive buildings almost everywhere in the city, magnificent temples with altars and statues and other monuments which today bear witness to that golden age, and to the various civilisations that evolved on the island.

THE PLAN OF THE CITY

1. Hotel Xenia
2. Ferry Terminal
3. Forest Inspection
4. Police Station
5. Telephone Office
6. Commercial Bank
7. KTEL Bus Station
8. National Bank
9. Post Office
10. Basilica
11. Museum
12. Port
13. The Temple of Dionysos
14. Ancient Agora
15. School
16. Ancient Odeion
17. Karakalla Arch
18. Health Centre
19. The Temple of Hercules
20. The Entrance of Satyros
21. Public Power Corporation
22. Agricultural Bank

Construction started on the **modern town** *(Limenas) in the mid-nineteenth century, with the work being carried out chiefly by inhabitants of the neighbouring village of Panaghia and other villages, all of whom gradually moved closer to the coast.*

In 1922 large numbers of refugees from Asia Minor and Thrace settled in the town, making a substantial contribution to the development and progress of the island. Life in Thasos today is centred on its attractive capital. It may be larger and more modern than the island's smaller villages but it lacks none of their picturesque charm. It is situated in the northern part of the island amid lush green mountains and hills. It is blessed with velvet-smooth beaches and countless ancient monuments, which require at least a day to see properly.

It is ideal for walks, for strolling in the narrow lanes with their dozens of exquisite little shops where you can find wonderful crafts and other goods. Also impressive are the colourful ouzo tavernas (ouzeri) *with their seafood appetizers, as tasty as any to be found in Greece. The town possesses a wide range of stores, easily covering all the needs both of visitors and of permanent residents. As for accommodation, there is a wide range of hotels, bungalows and rooms for rent that are open almost all year round.*

From May to October, in particular, Thasos town pulses with life. Greek and international visitors can enjoy great variety in their holidays, with Thasos abundantly catering for all preferences.

Today's Thasian houses, standing amid ruins that recall an ancient civilisation, provide a rich hint of the atmosphere on the island. Quiet, much-frequented beaches during the day day alternate with a lively nightlife to satisfy every age and mood.

Limenas is unquestionably the best point of departure for anyone planning to set out on a tour of the island aiming to become acquainted with every last corner of this paradise on earth. Equally indisputable is the beauty of the town harbour, which has ferry-boat and hydrofoil connections with the ports of Keramoti and Kavala on the mainland opposite.

The modern town of Limenas has many attractions.

It is quite sizeable and is located alongside what remains of the ancient port, now used mostly by fishermen. Commercial vessels call all year round at the harbour, which is also ideal for evening walks. As summer approaches, the port begins to hum with life and the shops there are soon crowded with people.

But you'll be glad to know that near all this bustling activity are the lovely, clean beaches of Limenas (photo 1), Glyfada and Glyfoneri (photo 3) which are ideal for swimming and just relaxing on days when you may be tired of exploring.

Limenas (photo 2) is a charming tourist resort combining peace and quiet with natural beauty and elegance. It deserves its status as capital of Thasos, giving visitors a taste of the unforgettable experiences they will subsequently enjoy as they get to know the rest of the island.

1

2

3

Archaeological Museum of Thasos:

The museum houses a wealth of fine collections covering the period from the 7th century BC to the 7th century AD. It should be pointed out from the outset that a good many important works of art from antiquity are also scattered around museums abroad. The phenomenon of the "transfer" of the ancient treasures of Thasos was extremely prevalent during the period of Ottoman rule. A firman from the sultan was enough to enable visitors to the island, upon departure, to take with them ancient artifacts that were lying about on the ground.

This was how the "Philis" stele and the famous relief plaque from the Pathway of the Ambassadors ended up in the Louvre Museum. Likewise, the twin brother of the eagle to be seen in the courtyard of the Thasos museum is now in Alexandria. Other ancient works can be found in a private collection in Vienna. At the end of the nineteenth century the finest pieces were shipped to Constantinople to form the nucleus around which the imperial Ottoman Museum was built. This dispersal of the ancient treasures of Thasos came to an end in 1912-1913.

The tour of the museum and its grounds starts as soon as the visitor finds himself in the courtyard of the museum. Two statues are there, vigilant watchmen and imposing witnesses to another age. One of them represents a lion (photo. 2) holding in his forepaws the head of an ox. This statue was found in the region of the ancient cemetery, near the tower of Sotas, and is probably part of a grave monument from the third century BC. The second is a larger statue of an eagle (photo 1), half-completed, which was found in the entrance to the Agora and dates from the Roman period. One can also find inscriptions, architectural fragments and works of sculpture including a large human torso found in the sanctuary of Hercules. Inside, the museum contains a large number of exhibits from different periods, fashioned in a variety of styles and techniques by artists and architects from Thasos and elsewhere. The marble and carved stone found in excavations of buildings testify to the variety and originality of architectural ornamentation on Thasos. Capitals, exquisitely carved anthemia and large numbers of plaques from pre-classical antiquity are all in

1

2

the Ionic order which was introduced to Thasos from Paros, homeland of the island's colonists, or from the neighbouring coasts. In many of the exhibits dating from the Archaic to the Roman period, the chief building material is the local marble, which is white or ash-coloured.

There are a number of sculptures in the Museum from the Archaic period. The most impressive is the ram-bearing Kouros (photo 3), 3.50m in height. Representing the donor or Apollo himself and dating from around 600 BC, it was found in the Pythion where it had been used as building material. The 1.23-high bust of Pegasus (photo 4) was created by the hand of a great artist in about 500 BC. The classical sculptures are also of exceptional quality, with the statue of Comedy, 1.70 in height, being particularly distinctive. On its pedestal it has an inscription which reads: "Comedy. Philemon was an actor." It is a male torso in a forceful stance, found in the Heracleion and is in the style of Pythagoras of Rhegium. Also noteworthy is the bas-relief of Hermes and the Graces, 0.44 cm high, which adorned one of the city gates, and the great funeral relief, 1.67 metres high, found in the necropolis of Pataria, dating from before 300 BC.

The exhibits in the Archaeological Museum of Thasos trace the island's history.

3

4

5

From the Hellenistic period (3rd-1st century BC) there are fine sculptures such as that of Dionysus, 2.20m in height, and the 1.82 metre-high Veiled Muse (photo 3). Both date from the first half of the 3rd century BC There is also "Aphrodite and the Dolphin" (photo 10), a type of statue intended for the interior of buildings. The facial features, the hairstyle and the perfection of the nude body recall the famous Aphrodite of Cnidus, a masterpiece by Praxiteles.

Headless statues of Nemesis (photo 4) were found between the market and the Odeion. The 2.10 metre-high statue of Hadrian was found in the vaulted chamber of the Agora or marketplace. A large number of Christian sculptures were also unearthed. An early Christian bas-relief depicting a peacock was found during the excavations of the basilicas of Alyki. Also worthy of note are the many impressive terracotta idols preserved in the museum after being discovered in the necropolis and in the marketplace. The most significant groups of them come from the sanctuary of Artemis and from Evraiokastro.

A substantial number of urns have come to light that had been manufactured by potters for the wine-export trade. Many urns similar to those of Thasos have also been discovered in Macedonia, Thrace, the Black Sea area, Egypt and Sicily, and as far away as the heart of Asia. The collection of silver and bronze coins from the 6th, 5th, 4th and 1st centuries has also won many admirers. The coins (photo 2) represent the heads of Dionysus and Hercules, a bust of Artemis and the abduction of a nymph by

1

Silenus. Finally, among the most important exhibits are the Museum's inscriptions; the ones displayed here represent a very small proportion of those found during the excavations. These inscriptions provide information about the history and the cultural and religious institutions of Thasos.

2

3

4

The Limenas archaeological site

Having lived through a glorious period which left behind it a truly magnificent archaeological heritage, Thasos is an ideal place for visitors who are admirers of the ancient world and everything that reminds them of it. Large numbers of visitors, including many scholars, come to the island each year to see and admire its outstanding ancient monuments.

During the hot summer months, the most suitable time for a walking tour of the ancient sites, which takes about two and a half hours, is in the morning. It is an easy, pleasant walk, enabling visitors to view in sequence all the outdoor monuments. The most suitable starting point is the old harbour in front of the museum. This archaeological walking tour is sure to remain in your memory because it combines the magic of the ancient monuments with the beauty of the lush, green landscape.

The ancient harbour

The harbour of Thasos was located on one of the great sea routes of the ancient world. It was used as a landing place in ancient times and retained its importance throughout history.

In effect there are two harbours. One of them, the "open" harbour, extended northwards from the rocks at the edge of Evraiokastro, along with a breakwater. It was protected from even the strongest winds. The breakwater facing the sea was fortified with a circular tower, with another two circular towers in the southwest protecting the "closed" harbour. There was so much traffic in the harbour in those distant times that it became necessary to install boundary markers. This is referred to in a 3rd century BC inscription preserved in the Archaeological Museum. The same inscription mentions that small boats were banned from entering the former harbour and large boats from going

PLAN OF ANCIENT AGORA

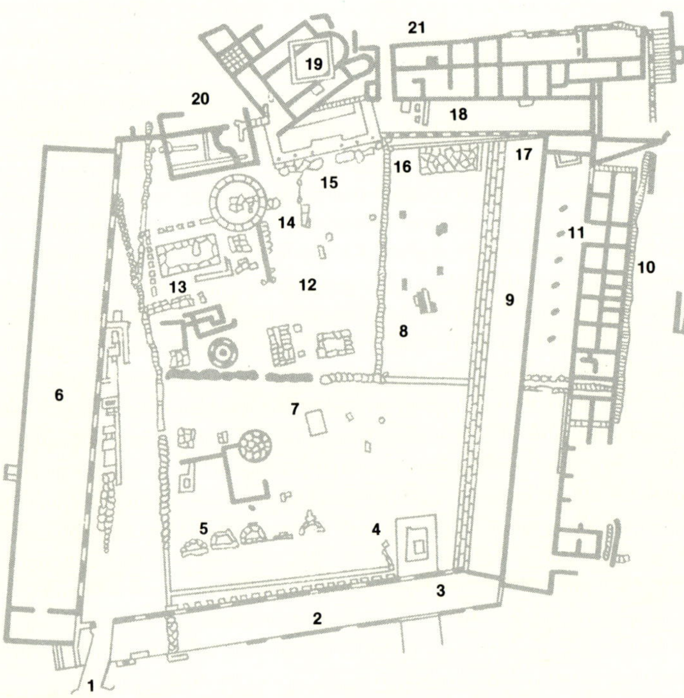

1. Entrance
2. Southwest gate
3. Monumental entrance
4. Monumental altar
5. Podium
6. Northweast gate
7. Drainage system
8. Altar of Theogenis
9. Southeast gate
10. Houses
11. Gallery
12. Temple of Julius Caesar
13. Temple of Zeus
14. Tholos
15. Law Courts
16. Base of statue of Victory
17. Northeast gate
18. Shops
19. Basilica
20. Public Building
21. Path

into the latter. Communication between the closed harbour and the market district was secured by three gates situated in the southeast, the centre and the northeast.

The ancient Agora

Near the old harbour behind the plane trees lies the civil and religious centre of the ancient city of Thasos: its Agora. This heart of the Thasian city-state once pulsed with life and was a political and commercial centre, a meeting place for men of leisure, merchants and entrepreneurs. The entrance to the Agora is opposite the Museum, with its forecourt in front of us. An ancient road led here from a gate in the outer wall, beside the harbour. The Agora is an open square about eighty by one hundred metres and is surrounded by buildings on all sides. It was founded some time around the 6th century BC. In the 4th century, a magnificent town plan was drawn up whose outline is still visible in the ruins on the site. Reconstruction, which started at the beginning of the 4th century BC, continued up to Roman times. The arcades, the sanctuaries, the altars, the buildings, the commemorative monuments, were built in succession one after another without any unifying concept. Around the arcades there are gates and passageways facilitating communication with the entire region around the town. In the Agora one can still see the remains of a section of the medieval fortifications, crowned with pine trees and surrounded by a moat, which in those days was full of water. To the south, the horizon opens out towards the distant peak of the Profitis Ilias, a suitable backdrop for the striking silhouette of the church of Aghios Nikolaos, built in 1835 out of materials from the ancient buildings.

The entrance to the ancient Agora or marketplace.

There are many other interesting monuments around the Agora, the most important of which are the following:

The **northwest arcade***, dating from the 3rd century BC. It was probably the offices of those dignitaries responsible for commercial administration and the management of the town finances.*

The **southwest arcade***, a building from a later period, dating from the 1st century AD and erected by two brothers Euphrillus and Micas, sons of Satyrus.*

The **podium***, which dates from the late 2nd century or early 1st century BC.*

The **main altar***, a work of the 3rd century BC.*

The **tomb of Glaucus***, friend of the poet Archilochus, which is probably the most ancient monument in the Agora, having been built in the second half of the 7th century.*

The **marble prow** *of a ship ploughing the waves.*

The **building with lobby***, a building constructed on the site of an earlier edifice and serving some aspect of public policy. It seems most likely to have been a law court of the 4th century BC.*

The **Temple of Zeus of the Agora***, one of the oldest structures in the Agora of Thasos, also built in the early 4th century BC.*

The **circular sanctuary of Theogenis** *or Theagenis, an Olympic champion who won over 1,300 athletic contests, dates from before the 2nd century BC.*

The **early Christian basilica of the Agora***, built in the 4th century AD, three-aisled with offertory and narthex, about 23.5 metres in length.*

Views of the ancient marketplace with the sanctuary of Theogenis to the right.

The Medieval Fortress

The Medieval fortress was built by the Grand Primikirios John at the end of the 14th century, a point mentioned in his will, which is in the archives of the Pantokrator monastery on Mount Athos. During the period in which the fortress was built, the inhabitants had abandoned the plain and taken refuge in the pass between the two peaks of the acropolis. It was therefore designed exclusively for the defence of the harbour. It is quite likely that between the central part of the fortress and the ruined tower there was a ditch, similar to the one separating the fortress proper from its eastern section. At the centre of the fortress stood a square building inside which there was a strange hall, distinctive in appearance and consisting of a rectangular space flanked on the north and south by two archways and with the entrance most likely from the eastern side. This building of indeterminate function must have been constructed around the end of the 5th century AD and was incorporated into the medieval fortress. Turning back to the entrance we descend to the level of the ancient market and find ourselves on the road that linked the market and the harbour. This was one of the most important traffic arteries of the ancient town. It was unpaved and maintenance work on it from the 4th century never consisted of anything more than adding landfill.

The Sanctuary of Theogenis

One of the most important monuments in the Agora square was the Sanctuary of Theogenis, who was among the most celebrated of Thasian athletes, with countless sporting victories to his credit. The sanctuary now consists of a circular base with some marble steps. A large quantity of ash and remains from sacrifices were found in the vicinity. In the centre of the Thasos Agora stood a miracle-working statue of Theogenis. Fragments were found there of the column on which was carved a record of the athlete's victories. A marble "thesaurus" (hollow cylinder) was also found, into which devotees cast their offering before the sacrifice. Inscriptions from the 2nd century BC are engraved on it.

Limenas.

Roman district - Podium - Odeion

Near the Agora is the great thoroughfare which was the town's central artery. It linked the centre and the Pathway of the Ambassadors with the district around the sanctuary of Hercules. In the section of the road near the Agora an ancient marble-paved road surface was unearthed along with a culvert by the wayside for collecting rain water. On the southeastern edge of the road was the podium constructed by the local sculptor Limentas, son of Haropinus, for the Thasian Tiberius Claudius Cadmus in the 1st century AD. Limentas also added a decorative element to this podium, carving on it sculptures of the family of Tiberius Cadmus. Behind the pedestal on three separate levels, a semicircular wall can still be seen with an inscription on it and crowned by an Ionic entablature, with an ox head and garlands on the frieze. The courtyard was laid out in the 2nd century AD and paved with 100 marble slabs. It was surrounded by an Ionic peristyle with twenty columns. Significant sections of the superstructure such as the bases of columns, lion's heads, etc. have been preserved. Beside the courtyard is a monument which has been identified as an odeion *or small theatre. This marble edifice still preserves the distinguishing features of a Greek theatre, such as the* orchestra *which takes up two-thirds of the circle, although other features of the edifice belong to the Roman era. The building dates from the 2nd century AD, the period of Hadrian's rule, when the whole area was reorganised.*

Pathway of the Ambassadors

The great arterial road leading from the Herakleion passes behind a building complex comprising shops and storehouses whose floor plan forms a regular network of quadrangles. Apart from the many inscriptions found inside the structure, numerous other inscriptions were discovered along with three cult bas-reliefs of a religious character depicting Apollo with Nymphs and Hermes with the Graces. They are to be found today in the Louvre. Two of the inscriptions provide information about the formal aspect of the religious ceremony. The inscription to Apollo and the Nymphs reads:

«To the Nymphs and to Apollo, leader of nymphs, you may sacrifice a male or female animal if you wish. Ewes and hogs are not permitted. No triumphal hymn is to be sung".

The other, which mentions the Graces, specifies that:

«Noone is permitted to sacrifice either a goat or a pig to the Graces".

The Pathway of the Ambassadors was one of the most important places in the ancient city, a place of great religious significance. Some of the findings, such as the altar to Athena at the Gate, point to the great respect in which the site was held. It was moreover situated on the sacred route followed by processions on their way up to the temple of Pythian Apollo and to the Acropolis.

*At the end of the 4th century BC the names of the Ambassadors (*Theoroi*) of Thasos were inscribed on the walls of the pathway. Near the Pathway of the Ambassadors is a large rectangular communal well, whose walls are constructed of marble and slate to a great depth.*

The Artemision

The sanctuary of Artemis, referred to as the Artemision in Hippocrates' "Epidemics", is situated above a chamber approximately 35 metres long where pure spring water once welled up out of the rock. The sanctuary is east of the Agora and was discovered in 1909 when, quite by chance, seven statues of women were found; they are now in the Museum in Istanbul. They were designed to honour certain distinguished women of Thasos and dedicated to Artemis by their husbands, sons or even by the municipality.

On the pedestal of one of them the signature of the Rhodian sculptor Philiscus Polyharmus can be discerned. Most of the artifacts that have come to light are objects used by women and dedicated to the goddess Artemis, who was their protector. They include decorative items in gold, bronze and ivory for adorning mirrors, lamps, vases, etc.

Statue of Dionysus in the sanctuary bearing his name.

All these objects date from the 7th and the early 5th centuries BC and show how important the cult of Artemis was to Greeks at the dawn of the pre-Classical era.

The Dionysion

To the north of the Pathway of the Ambassadors is the sanctuary of Dionysus (called the Dionysion by Hippocrates). The overall plan of the sanctuary became clear in the course of exploratory excavations that were carried out from time to time but were gradually covered over again. Nevertheless, the position of at least two entrances was ascertained as well as an enclosing wall constructed from blocks of marble and apparently dating from the 4th century BC. The temple, located in the western section of the sanctuary, with modern buildings on top of it, has yet to be explored.

In the area of the sanctuary, two important choragic monuments were found from the theatrical contests presided over by Dionysus as lord of the theatre. The foundations of one monument date from the beginning of the third century; its two statues, one of Dionysus and one of a Muse, are to be found in the museum. The second monument dates from the second half of the 4th century and was mounted on a podium with stairs on the facade because the terrain at this point makes access difficult. The building was fronted by a portico with four Doric columns and behind the colonnade is a base descibing an arch. On it stood the statue of Dionysus, larger than life-size, with eight smaller statues around it. Among the best-known finds are the head of Dionysus, the headless statue of Comedy, its base, which has no inscription, and the mask which was the emblem of Tragedy. All of these are to be found on exhibit in the Museum.

The Posideion

Northwest of the Dionysion, following a narrow road which winds among houses and orchards, there appears before us the surrounding wall of a sanctuary with fine regular stonework from the Classical era. It encloses an irregular quadrangle of land that extends to the foot of a rocky slope. Proceeding into the main courtyard, we can see three structures side by side: a circular altar covered with slate; another altar in the shape of the letter Π, flanked by pilasters. These two altars were used to serve the needs of the person offering the sacrifice. A third rectangular structure may have functioned as the foundation of some small shrine.

A Hellenistic inscription found on the site confirms the existence of a society of Poseidonians which held common symposia. Poseidon was not the only god to have been worshipped and/or honoured in this sanctuary, as evidenced by a statuette representing a female deity seated on a dolphin, the Aphrodite Pelagia or Amphitrite. Finally, to the right of the main entance an altar was found. The sanctuary of Poseidon dates from the 4th century BC.

The Gate of the Goddess in the Chariot

Proceeding along the road that leads us to the edge of Evraiokastro and following the line of the ancient wall to just before the harbour, we come to a rather well-preserved gate. This gate opens towards the northwest, interrupting the solid marble barrier of the wall. It is situated right between the two ancient harbours near the point at which the wall became the northern defences of the "closed harbour". The locks on the gate are still in very good condition, and on the door-frame one can see the holes in which the cross bars fitted, thus securing the door. On the pilaster over the threshold there is a bas-relief dating from the beginning of the 5th century, representing a goddess coming out of the city on a chariot drawn by two horses. The goddess is a young girl with her hair tied back and dressed in traditional Ionian costume, a tunic and a pleated mantle. Beside the horses walks a bearded man in a robe, holding the animals by the reins. The goddess is Artemis and the bearded figure the god Hermes. One finds similar relief plaques, which serve a protective function, at most gates in the wall.

The Gate of Hermes and the Graces

Beyond the Gate of the Goddess in the Chariot, as we go forward alongside the wall about 150 to the north, there is an entire ancient quarter situated behind the city wall. Inside the wall was a road that ran parallel to it. Descending to that level we can see the side of the wall that looks over the city. The city gate in this district went through two stages of construction. The bas-relief still to be seen on the pilaster to the right belongs to the first period and dates from the first half of the 5th century BC To the right of the relief, a male figure can be seen, nude apart from the robe hanging loosely from his shoulders, proceeding towards the interior of the city, with three other figures, female and clothed, following him. This divine procession is identifiable as Hermes walking in front of his companions, the Graces. In the 4th century BC, the foundations of the passage were raised, the threshold was covered over and the pilasters were put back in a new, higher, position.

The open harbour

After the Gate of Hermes, just up from the wall, the present-day road climbs uphill. The open harbour is situated a little before the end of the wall, a branch of which used to continue about a hundred metres further into the sea.

Evraiokastro

On a headland outside the fortress there was once an early Christian church, occupying the site of an earlier ancient sanctuary that had been erected on a level area on the rocks, on a landfill terrace. The 5th century basilica has a narthex paved with re-used ancient marble, and flanking the narthex is a rectangular chamber with a circular ancillary area dating from the same period.

During the Byzantine period, following the destruction of the church, all the area around the building was taken up by a cemetery, forty of whose graves have been excavated. The artifacts which have been unearthed were almost all found in the landfill below the large retaining wall. They mainly consist of earthenware statuettes and inscriptions which testify to cults of Zeus, Athena, Artemis, the Nymphs and Persephone (Kore). The climb from Evraiokastro up to the Acropolis is not particularly difficult, as one follows the wall, which is still in remarkably good condition. In its lower section, some remnants of masonry with curved joints can still be seen. So, following this route we finally arrive at the top of the rise where the theatre is situated.

The archaeological site of Evraiokastro is of special interest.

The ancient theatre

The ancient theatre lies in a natural hollow of the hill against the wall. Its seats are shaded by pine trees and, as we learn from Hippocrates, they have been in exactly the same place since the 5th century BC. The foundations discovered beneath the stage date from the time of Hegemon, the Thasian actor and comic writer whom Aristotle regarded as being the inventor of parody. The marble facade of the stage was built at the beginning of the 3rd century BC. It was then that the proscenium was dedicated to Dionysus by the Thasian Lysistratus, son of Codes. In the same period theatrical productions flourished, with choragic monuments dedicated to Dionysus. The celebrations were organised by a number of different foreign artists such as Ariston of Miletus, who played the flute. From the 1st century AD the theatre was used for "hunting" and gladiatorial games. The high priests of the cult of the emperor maintained professional fighters such as mirmillones *(gladiators armed in helmet, sword and shield),* retiarii *(net men),* essedarii *(chariot men). Gladiatorial contests also took place between pairs of men on horseback, while the orchestra was transformed into an arena and the side-streets were closed with heavy doors. Subsequently, towards the end of the 2nd century AD, Heragoras, the son of Euphrillus, erected parapets with iron balustrades at the level of the lower aisles to isolate the spectators.*

During the same period some important alterations were also made to the stage building. In the centre of the colonnades metopes were carved to represent the gods that were then in favour: Dionysus treating his panther to wine from a kantharos *drinking cup, and Ares with helmet and breastplate are just two of the subjects depicted. Some gladiators also carved bas-reliefs of Nemesis on the walls of the stage building which were discovered in 1887 and have been in the Istanbul Museum since then.*

The Acropolis

We come out of the theatre to find ourselves on the same path. Following the line of the wall we arrive at a long, narrow stretch of level ground which provided ancient and then Byzantine architects with an ideal site for the construction of a citadel or Acropolis (photo 1,2). As a site it was superbly well-chosen because it was an excellent lookout point, 137 metres above the level of the sea. In its present-day form, the citadel dates from medieval times, though there is one corner of the wall constructed of large blocks of marble, that has come down from the Acropolis of the 5th century BC, when settlers introduced the cult of Apollo, an event confirmed by inscriptions found here. The initial ground plan of the 5th century BC Acropolis was slowly effaced with the passage of time and with the succession of modifications that took place in the Middle Ages. The only buildings on the Acropolis today are two towers, two water cisterns and the ruined chapel with the semicircular archway, that dates from the time of the Gateluzzi.

The Sanctuary of Athena

Following the path that crosses the ruins of the medieval village, we come to the second summit of the Acropolis, the site of an ancient sanctuary. Its identity was confirmed by the potsherds and urns found on this spot with the name of Athena, protector of the city, incised upon them. The sanctuary was situated on a broad terrace. Excavations have revealed the ruins of a temple, razed to its foundations, which was constructed with huge hewn stones joined at the corners by bolts in the shape of a double T.

This monumental complex of temple buildings and its terrace, which can be dated to the early 5th century BC, is the successor to a more ancient sanctuary. Inside the 5th-century temple some badly built foundations still survive, testifying to the existence of an older building. The most interesting of the artifacts found during excavations of the sanctuary were terracotta statuettes, vessels, votive plates and decorative antefixa from the older temple.

1

2

The Sanctuary of Pan

Following the path along the walls which leads from the Sanctuary of Athena to the third peak on the Acropolis, we pass in front of the sanctuary of the god Pan, hewn out of the rock. There is a bas-relief in a pediment-like border decorating the cave. In its centre is the goat-footed god playing his pipes, with three nanny-goats on the left listening to him. The main thematic element at the top of the pediment consists of two male goats standing on a kantharos *drinking cup and butting their heads together. Rectangular niches have been carved into the rock into which votive offerings or a cult statue of the god may have been placed.*

The Wall and Gate of Parmenon

Having climbed up past the cave containing the sanctuary of Pan, we come to the precipitous southern summit of the Acropolis with its jagged peak. This peak merges into the terrace of temple of Athena with its wall to the east of the cave of Pan. The fortified wall, constructed of ashlar masonry, descends once again to the plain, following the line of the steepest part of the hillside and is attached to the rocky ridge by means of a two-storeyed tower, whose interior staircase is to this day the only means of descent. Some metres farther down, the fortifications make a right-angle turn. Just before we get to this point there is a large rock with two eyes and a nose, carved to look like a face. This is a magic image giving the wall the power to protect against the evil eye. (The evil eye or matiasma: According to folk beliefs, this means "to affect adversely by looking at someone/thing, to cause harm by a glance, either by reason of jealousy or by the expression of admiration). Farther down still, another large rock in the wall bears an inscription which must have been carved between 510 and 490 BC, probably by a stone mason, and says: "Parmenon made me". At a yet lower point there is a gate, whose lintel is still preserved. It consists of a huge piece of slate supported on large pilasters.

The Gate of Hercules and Dionysus

Following the wall in the direction of the sea we reach the gate of Hercules and Dionysus, dating from the early 5th century. An entrance was cut through the rugged masonry of the marble wall. On either side of the entrance inside, there were two buttresses, while the pilasters flanking the gate and its threshold were situated more or less on the point where the path crossed inside of the wall. This entrance was protected by the two great gods of Thasos, Dionysus and Hercules.

The Ancient Necropolis

On the plain, beyond the gates and as far as the lower mountain slopes, lies the ancient necropolis (=city of the dead) or cemetery. Many monuments have been found in it, including large Roman sarcophagi, one of which, that of Poliades, dates from the 3rd century BC.

The sculptures and inscriptions from the various periods are also interesting. Many of the grave steles are carved, such as the 6th century BC stele with a seated female figure smelling a flower; the stele of Philis, which is now situated in the Louvre and dates from the 5th century BC, and the stele of Phaedra from the 4th century BC. Among the subjects depicted in bas relief are numerous scenes of funeral suppers, e.g. those from the 5th century BC, and Thracian riders, from the 2nd century BC. Carved on a number of the steles are inscriptions dedicated to the deceased. Research carried out in the area in 1952-53 revealed a great number of Greek graves and an edifice which is clearly the shrine of a hero. Apart from the large numbers of votive offerings discovered among the graves, bronze and silver Thasian coins from the 4th century BC were also found, as well as a significant collection of silver coins from the same period originating from the cities of Byzantium and Chalcedon.

The Heracleion

The Heracleion was one of the most important temples on Thasos, Hercules being the island's most important god, and protector of the city. According to the tradition passed on to us by Herodotus, the cult of Hercules was brought to Thasos by the Phoenicians. Excavations have brought to light the greater part of this sanctuary, of which the monumental entrance is in good condition and consists of a propylaea, or gateway, a double Doric facade, and a broad staircase. The propylaea and facade lead to a paved square in front of a large altar. The Heracleia, the god's great feast days, were distinguished for their military contests accompanied by a symposium, when the people of Thasos would assemble in front of this monumental sacrificial table. All the sanctuary buildings were situated around the square and consisted of an Ionic temple, a long, narrow pavilion, a row of rooms and the "household" building, to which a temple was added in the 6th century. A triangular courtyard was also unearthed in the area of the sanctuary with a circular monument in its centre.

TOUR OF THE ISLAND

Thasos is large enough to allow visitors to organise their excursions to reflect the mood of the moment. Besides, there's such a variety of sights to see on the island that even the shortest tour offers something of special interest. The following pages describe two itineraries that we believe will offer a relaxing and pleasant tour, giving visitors a chance to enjoy some of the varied features of the island.

One itinerary covers the **northwestern section** of the island starting from Limenas, Thasos's main port, and ending at delightful Limenaria; the other covers **northeastern Thasos** starting from Makryammos and ending at the settlement of Theologos. Both these itineraries will take you along the coast road, although people who prefer mountains can also take excursions inland to explore Mount Ypsario. Here there are many hamlets, some of which are situated in rarely visited and remote places, and which constitute a point of reference for even the most demanding traveller. Moreover, in the port of Thasos, mainly in the summer, a number of travel agencies organise tours of the island, and sometimes a boat that starts out from Limenaria doing tours around Mount Athos.

We hope that this little book, together with own personal experience of the island, will ensure you a truly unforgettable vacation.

1ST ROUTE: ***Northwestern Thasos***

2ND ROUTE: ***Northeastern Thasos***

Don't miss:

MUSEUMS:
- The Archaeological Museum of Thasos with unique and varied collections from the period between the 7th century BC and the 7th century AD
- The Kallirachi Folk Museum housed in a lovely heritage mansion dating from 1880
- The Vaghis Museum, Skala Potamias

ARCHAEOLOGICAL SITES:
- The archaeological site in the town of Thasos with many interesting monuments that are described in detail in the chapter describing the ancient sites of Limenas
- Alyki with its ancient and medieval monuments
- The Castle in Potos where there is a necropolis and settlement

BEACHES:
- Prinos
- Skala Kallirachis
- Coastal settlement of Kallirachi
- Skala Marion
- The Tripiti beach and others at Limenaria
- The Psili Ammos beach at the southern tip of the island
- Pefkari
- Makryammos
- The Chrysi Ammoudia beach at Skala Potamias
- The Paradisos beach and others at Kinyra

MONASTERIES - COUNTRY CHURCHES:
- Monastery of Aghios Panteleimon at Skala Sotira
- Monastery of the Archangel Michael at Alyki
- Church of the Virgin Mary in Panaghia
- Chapel of the Aghii Anargyrii at Kallirachi
- Countryside Churches in Panaghia
  Aghios Athanasios
  Aghii Constantinos and Eleni
  Aghios Haralambos
  Aghios Ioannis

The archaeological site of Alyki.

5 NORTHW

Rachoni - Agios Georgios - Prinos - Kaza

This part of the island, with its charming mountain villages, attracts most of the visitors. Nor of course is there any shortage of splendid coasts with endless sandy beaches and shady forests clinging to the mountain slopes. Almost directly opposite Thasos on the mainland are the towns of Keramoti, Kavala and Nea Peramos. Rachoni, Prinos, Kazaviti, Sotiras, Kallirachi, Maries, Limenaria and Pefkari are located in northwestern Thasos.

STERN THASOS

Skala Sotira - Kallirachi - Maries - Limenaria

Many of these mountainous villages have a *skala* or dock on the coast; but these are only busy during the summer months. For the rest of the year, the majority of the inhabitants live in land.

Aerial view of Limenaria.

1

2

Rachoni - Aghios Georgios

After Limenas and Glyfada, one of the island's seasonal tourist resorts, is the community of Rachoni (photo 1,2). This is one of the quieter and more remote villages on Thasos and consists of the village of Rachoni itself, Skala Rachoniou, and the nearby small village of Aghios Georgios (photo 3).
In the past, most of the residents of Aghios Georgios and Rachoni lived farther inland for fear of pirates, and it was only when that danger had finally passed that they came down and settled nearer the coast.

Muhammad Ali, founder of the dynasty that ruled Egypt from the 19th to the early 20th century, was raised in this old village before moving on to Kavala on the mainland. Skala Rachoniou, like the other skalas on the island is more oriented to tourism with accommodation and restaurants.

The mountain villages provide an alternative to people visiting Thasos.

3

Prinos

Following the discovery of oil and the installation of oil-drilling platforms off its coast, Prinos became one of the most important places on the island. The village community includes Prinos (also known as Kalivia), the new settlement of Prinos and Skala Prinou. Prinos is a mountain village, its coastal offshoot, Skala Prinou, is within easy reach of Kavala on the mainland by ferry and hydrofoil. The new settlement of Prinos is on a site of unique natural beauty, and is the most developed spot as regards tourist facilities. It has endless sandy beaches, whose clear waters merge with the green forest to create the illusion that the pine trees have risen out of the sea. Prinos also has luxury hotels and rooms to rent to accommodate its many summer visitors.

Prinos is the second port of Thasos.

Kazaviti

Following the road that begins from the present day village of Prinos we arrive at Kazaviti. Built on a wooded hillside at the end of a valley, it is among the island's most picturesque villages. Unfortunately today it is almost deserted, the old stone houses with their wooden porches and painted ceilings are still standing but are barely visible through the dense greenery. In the past the village was divided into Mikro (= small) Kazaviti and Megalo (=large) Kazaviti, which in the last century were called Papazmachala and Tsigoura respectively. At the time when mountain villages had more inhabitants and were more developed, Kazaviti also had its days of glory. In fact, a fairly significant school operated in Megalo Kazaviti which contributed greatly to the area. Today one can visit modern Kazaviti and admire what has remained of the school and old mansions. Nature has been generous in this area, and picturesque Kazaviti is one of the first places on Thasos that tourists visit. The little coffee shops surrounded by lush greenery make it all the more inviting.

The green background and stone houses of Kazaviti will remain in your memory.

Skala Sotira

The village of Sotiras is situated in the interior of the island, on the slopes of Ypsario, at an altitude of 300 metres and is perfect for summer vacations. The climate is among the best on the island and the surrounding area is quite lovely. Skala Sotira is built along the length of the nearby lovely serene seashore. In Roman times there were in fact baths here and the area was known for its restful atmosphere. Today, Skala Sotira has been greatly developed with hotels and rooms to rent. Even so, it remains one of the most peaceful spots on the island. Of great interest is also the monastery of Aghios Panteleimon which is accessible by a steep uphill road through forested hillsides.

Kallirachi - Skala Kallirachis

Kallirachi is one of the island's leading villages and is divided into two communities, the upland and the coastal one. The upland part is built on a mountain slope and is the seat of the village authorities (local council, police).

The folk museum is a notable feature of the village. It is housed in a beautifully preserved heritage mansion dating from the 1880's which also serves as a cultural centre. The village is surrounded by olive groves and has a fine dry climate. Just a kilometre outside the village is the well known chapel of Aghii Anarghyrii situated in an enchanting landscape. The chapel is the site of a number of miracles, and its proximity gives the inhabitants strength and courage.

Skala Sotira.

1

About 2.5 kilometres down from the upland village is the coastal settlement built along the seashore. The beach, with its clean waters, is delightful and easily accessible. There is a good range of tourist accommodation and entertainment as well as quaint shops.

Kallirachi seems to attract many tourists who arrive by road or hydrofoil (the so-called "Flying Dolphins") from Kavala.

1. The village of Kallirachi.
2, Skala Kallirachis.

2

Maries - Skala Marion

The medieval village of Maries retains its old character. It stands at a high point in a ravine, its houses built closely together for reasons of safety and economy. The houses had ornamental brackets under on the balconies and in the interior sitting room, and magnificent carved screens and ceilings. There are Byzantine records relating to the village in the monastic community on Mount Athos. Some of the monasteries there had close ties with Maries and its inhabitants which lasted until 1926. In the region of the village there are three Mount Athos monastery dependencies. One belongs to the monastery of Stavronikita, the second to Karakallou and the third to Xiropotamou.

*According to the oral tradition there are two versions of how the village got its name. The first is that the name refers to mulberry trees (*mouries*) which are plentiful in the area, while the second attributes the name to the tale of two women called Maria whose lives were spared after a pirate raid on their village ended in the death of almost all its inhabitants. About 13 kilometres from the upland village is the coastal settlement of Skala Marion. It offers a beautiful coastline with crystal waters, and despite being one of the lesser known beaches on the island, it can get quite crowded in summer.*

Limenaria

After Skala Marion, the coastal road leads to Limenaria. This is a large village that came into being at the end of the 19th century, at the expense of the nearby medieval fortress-village which is situated on a plateau inland. The harbour of Limenaria began to gain commercial importance in 1903 when a large foreign firm used it to load the ores it had extracted from the area onto ships. The imposing company office building, long since abandoned, still stands in the picturesque fishing harbour. The current development of the village is due chiefly to tourism.

During the summer months Limenaria and its pretty white-pebble beaches attract many visitors. A collection of antiquities, housed in the small village museum, is also of interest to tourists.

Left page: Skala Marion, one of the island's attractions.
Right page: The port of Limenaria.

Limenaria.

In the middle of a large valley of olive groves inland from Limenaria, is the small village of **Kalivia** *Limenarion. Ancient stone bas reliefs that have been incorporated into the walls of the local church bear witness to the existence of a much earlier settlement in the area.*

Near Limenaria is the beach of **Tripiti**, *a wonderful stretch of sandy coast with sparkling blue waters. The surrounding scenery, as in much of Thasos, is verdant green and among the most impressive on the island. The beach here has no organised facilities, despite which fact it manages to attract a good many bathers who enjoy the sun and sea. Farther along, at the southern tip of the island is the* **Psili Ammos** *(=fine sand) beach which is yet another notable attraction. It spreads out directly below a small forested hillside, a sight which draws visitors like a magnet. The entire beach is of a brilliant white sand, perfect for sunbathing, while a rocky point nearby makes an ideal point for diving into the crystal clear waters. There are places for tents and caravans at Psili Amos as well as a picturesque taverna which is open all day.*

1

2

1, 2. The mines at Limenaria and the nearby beach.
3. The Tripiti beach.
4. The brilliant white beach of Psili Ammos.

3

4

Leaving Limenaria and the surrounding area and heading east, we come to **Pefkari**. *This is a picturesque settlement built among the pine trees in front of one of the most attractive beaches on Thasos. Visitors come here in large numbers so there's rented accommodation and a luxury hotel complex to provide a wide range of options to suit all tastes and pocketbooks. The beach at Pefkari, with lofty pine trees rising almost at the water's edge, is a sight to see. The water is the colour of the sky and the sand is warm and inviting. The beach has organised facilities to serve all bathers' needs.*

In Pefkari, the green pines merge with the sea.

6 NORTHEA

Makryammos - Panaghia - Chrysi Ammouc

One of the great features of Thasos is considered to be its unique natural beauty, the like of which can be found on no other island in the Aegean, or perhaps even in the entire country. The scenery is so magnificent that it leaves even the most experienced traveller spellbound. The whole island is covered with dense forests, caves, ravines, olive groves and lovely coastlines. The azure of the sky, deep blue of the sea and dark green of the pine forests combine to create scenery of rare beauty.

STERN THASOS

Potamia - Kinyra - Alyki - Astrida - Potos - Theologos

Although all the beaches are delightful, some sandy, others with fine pebbles and others rocky, there are some that stand out. Our tour begins with one such at Makryammos, and continues with Panaghia, Chrysi Ammoudia, Potamia, Kinyra, Paradisos, Alyki, the Monastery of the Archangel Michael, Astrida, Potos and finally Theologos.

The beach at Makryammos and the rock opposite.

Makryammos

Makryammos is a very pretty beach with clear waters in a picturesque bay bordered by pine trees to the east of the town of Limenas. The beach is sandy, with organised facilities, ideal for endless hours of sunbathing. To the right of the beach is a wharf, a shelter for small boats and pleasure craft. Right opposite, on the other side of the bay, is a small, pine-clad rock adding to the beauty of the surroundings.

There are tourist lodgings near the beach for visitors who wish to stay the night.

Makryammos.

Panaghia

Panaghia is a traditional Thasian village with a rich history, much of which is unfortunately unknown. Both the name of the village and its eleven countryside chapels (exokklesia) bear witness to the religious fervour of its inhabitants. Miracles have been attributed to these chapels, and it is true that they constituted places of refuge for Christians in hard times. The chapel of Aghios Athanasios, built in 1818, is outstanding, as are those of Aghii Constantinos and Eleni and Aghios Charalambos, built in 1825. Also notable is the chapel of Aghios Panteleimon and Aghios Georgios which was built in 1830, the chapel dedicated to the Beheading of John the Baptist, built in 1835, and the chapel of the Virgin Mary (Panaghia), built in 1845.

The **Church of the Virgin Mary** is also of interest, being closely associated with the cultural and economic life of the village. The history of this church is closely linked with the history of the village, although with some gaps, especially during the years after the fall of Constantinople (1453) and at the end of the 17th century. Unfortunately, the precise date the present church was built remains unknown. If we judge from the fact that the village took its name from the church then it must have been built before 1821, the year of the Greek War of Independence against the Ottoman Empire.

According to tradition, the church was consecrated by the Metropolitan Anthimos. In the 18th century the inhabitants of the ancient town of Thasos (present day Limenas) were forced by pirate raids to head for the interior of the island; they settled in Panaghia. Many more joined them when the Russian Fleet was stationed in the area in 1770. The significant increase in the town's population gave rise to the need for a larger church.

It is nice to relax at the village fountain and in the quaint little coffee shop.

Panaghia.

The church of Panaghia.

Work on the new church began in 1831 under the supervision of craftsmen from Kastoria on the mainland, who were skilled in ecclesiastical architecture. The money to begin the project was donated by the notables Sotirios Avgoustis, and Avgerinos and Chatzis Constantinos, whose tombstone is in the church precinct. However, as the funds were insufficient to complete this grand church, the village appealed to Mount Athos for help. The monastery of Vatopedi, which was the most robust financially, came to their aid. But to this day, the church has still not been built to its full height.

The wooden icon screen was carved by craftsmen from Volos in 1881. The artisans from Kastoria gave the church many features characteristic of the Byzantine churches in their own town. The dome is raised and octagonal, the apse over the sanctuary is a semi-octagon. The church, which is 27.5 metres long, 18.60 on wide and 18 m. high, was built with marble blocks from the area of Panaghia.

Pieces of marble from the ruins of the ancient temples on Thasos were also used in its construction. It is a three-aisled vaulted basilica, and on either side of the narthex there are small alcoves called griyitika (gria = old woman), in other words areas for elderly women.

The northern alcove is dedicated to Aghios Haralambos. The church has five entrances, the main western entrance and the others leading to the side aisles. It is dedicated to the Dormition of the Virgin, although there is an icon in the church depicting the Virgin, bearing an inscription dated 1814 and the title Pantavlepousa ("The all-seeing").

Chrysi Ammoudia

A few kilometres down from Panaghia is one of the island's best known beaches. Chrysi Ammoudia (=golden sands) appears to be a truly endless golden beach with fine sand which leaves the first-time visitor speechless. There are pine trees along the 3.5-km long bay and lodgings for tourists.

Chrysi Ammoudia has organised facilities for those who enjoy water sports and long hours of sunbathing.

One of the most beautiful spots on Chrysi Ammoudia, from which you can admire its entire expanse, is Vigli, a densely forested place above the beach where a picturesque taverna is situated, surrounded by cool greenery.

The lovely beach at Chrysi Ammoudia.

Potamia - Skala Potamias

Potamia is built on the foothills of Ypsario, the tallest mountain on Thasos, surrounded by the lush forest that is the main feature of the island. Starting from Potamia, one can climb to the summit of Ypsario along an especially pretty path through the greenery. Of interest in the village is a museum dedicated to the work of the renowned Thasian sculptor, Polygnotos Vaghis.

Skala Potamias is a short distance from the upland village and has beaches with crystal clear waters. The well-organised beach of Potamia is long and sandy, with shallow clean water that makes it ideal for families with children.

There are rooms for rent and other tourist accommodations along the beach, with tavernas and village shops nearby. The picturesque fishermen's wharf close to the beach is very pleasant for an evening stroll. The beach of Potamia attracts a fair number of visitors who prefer camping.

1. Skala Potamias.
2, 3. Vaghis Museum (phot. 2) in the village of Potamia (phot. 3).

1

2

3

Kinyra

Kinyra is one of the prettiest villages in eastern Thasos. Its name has been preserved in this location for centuries. Practically all the Kinyra region is scattered with artifacts and ruins from antiquity and the Middle Ages. The vegetation is lush due to the many springs in the surrounding hillsides, and it's considered one of the most favoured places on the island. In the old days, there were few permanent residents, mostly fishermen and shepherds, but the place filled with people at harvest time. Today the area is developing its tourist trade in leaps and bounds owing to its beautiful beaches and crystalline waters.

Off the coast there is a charming little island, also called Kinyra, whose shape resembles a mandolin or bouzouki. Its surface is almost entirely covered with pine and olive trees. It has rocky beaches and the sea around teems with fish of all kinds. The house and property of the person to whom the island originally belonged have been preserved. Visitors reach the island as they have always done, by boat.

Until recently, rare Mediterranean seals could also be seen in the surrounding waters. The area of Kinyra is known for its peace and quiet, and the wonderful scenery it has to offer, including **Paradisos** *beach. Access to this beach which, it should be noted, is one of the favourite tourist spots, is by a road that winds*

its way through a wooded area. The beach is not particularly long, but the forest around it and the fact that the sea is almost always pounding in with big breakers, make it reminiscent of an exotic tropical isle.

The water is a transparent green and certain points among the rocks often provide a retreat for nudists. The small forest directly above the beach is ideal for camping and is full of caravans and tents throughout the summer.

Green meets azure blue on the unique beaches of Thasos.

Alyki

Alyki is one of the most beautiful spots in all of Thasos, as well as being a site of great archaeological interest, with many ancient and medieval monuments. Right behind the shacks that stand on the beach today there was once a significant ancient settlement. In its heyday, the settlement was very prosperous, evidence of which can be seen in the surviving monuments. The most important of these are the sanctuary, the cult caves, and the marble quarries. The settlement of Alyki seems to have had its most prosperous period during the Middle Ages, judging from what remains of the two basilican churches from the Byzantine era built on a rise a short distance from the quarries.

Swimming with the vestiges of the past in the background.

Pirate raids in the 7th century AD appear to have forced the inhabitants to abandon the settlement and quarries.

*Until recently, Alyki was a beautiful but isolated corner of the Theologos region. The few remaining inhabitants were engaged in fishing, growing olives and extracting salt from the sea. Today this enchanting area of Thasos has been transformed. The shacks have been turned into little tavernas serving ouzo and appetizers (*ouzeri*) or grilled fish and meat (*psistaries*) to feed the thousands of tourists who flood into the area in the summer. The clear waters of the bay form a magnificent natural pool surrounded by ancient ruins hidden by the pine and olive trees. In the evening the still waters send up shimmering gold reflections from the gaily lit tavernas and boats moored in the bay.*

The beach at Alyki is a favourite among tourists and locals alike as it combines sand, pebbles, and rocks while the sea is so clear that one loses all sense of depth.

The green pine trees are reflected in sea waters on the enchanting beach at Alyki.

Of particular interest in the area is the nearby **monastery of the Archangel Michael**. It is the last of its kind on the island, founded by the monastery of Philotheou on Mount Athos. The establishment of this monastery is shrouded in legends and oral tradition. According to a rumour that circulated widely in 1923, the chapel of Michael the Archangel was built by a holy man named Loukas. The precise date of the monastery's foundation is not known. The monastery is first mentioned in an official document in 1287.

In 1835 some repairs were made and it seems most likely that the church was completed then. Today it is 9 metres long, 5 metres wide and 3 metres high. Moreover, in 1890 the priest-monk, Zosimas Philotheitis received permission from the monastery of Philotheou to build a small roof over the narthex of the church, and a small room. One of the treasures in the possession of the monastery of Michael the Archangel is a piece of one of the nails that were used in the crucifixion of Christ.

The unique grace surrounding this relic has given the monastery enormous prestige and attracted large numbers of pilgrims.

In order not to lose its rights over this holy relic, the monastery of Philotheou built a monastery dependency with a small chapel at Theologos. A monk, whom the locals called primatikos, was in permanent residence there. It was the custom in those days for the faithful to donate offerings to the church so that their names would be remembered. The God-fearing people of Theologos, in particular, showed their reverence towards the Archangel Michael by donating land, houses, and sometimes their entire fortunes, as a result of which the monastery acquired enormous wealth.

The monastery's ownership status changed in 1927, when an agrarian law was passed concerning the expropriation of monastery dependencies on Thasos and Limnos. Under this law the entire property of the monastery was divided between 72 landless families in 1931.

In October 1974, the first seven nuns arrived from the convent of the Virgin Hodegetria in Portaria, Volos, headed by their abbess, Ephremia.

Together with father Joseph, the priest-monk of Philotheou responsible for the monastery dependency at Theologos, they worked hard and transformed the monastery which had become terribly run down. Since then the monastery of Michael the Archangel has functioned as a coenobite women's hermitage, which is spiritually dependent on the monastery of Philotheou on Mount Athos.

To sum up, Alyki is a small earthly paradise, the like of which cannot be found in all of Greece.

The monastery of the Archangel is one of the highlights of Thasos while the beach below it is suitable for swimming.

Astrida

Astrida is a wide region full of farmland in the southeastern part of the island. Its name is derived from the Greek word for stars, because for most of the year, the sky above the flat land is ablaze with stars. It also has one of the healthiest climates on Thasos and the best water. Even though vegetation on the plain and surrounding mountains is very poor, Astrida is nevertheless beautiful. There has always been a small permanent settlement here of cottages belonging to those who kept livestock and grew olives. The ruins of ancient buildings and defensive towers can be seen. Today the area is full of modern hotels and night clubs ready to delight the visitor.

The sky is always clear at Astrida.

Potos

Potos was once one of the largest and most important settlements of cottages belonging the people of Theologos. It had the most permanent inhabitants, because it was closest to the village, the only settlement to be connected to it by road, and because it was the skala, in other words the port, of Theologos.

It was at Potos that the boat docked which connected the village with Kavala on the mainland. Those who lived in this settle-ment were either livestock farmers, fishermen, or boatmen. The latter rowed the travellers over to the caique which took them to Kavala or brought the arrivals to the village's sandy shore.

Today Potos is one of the best-known tourist resorts on the island with unprecedented development. There has been a frenzy of construction and business is booming. Splendid, luxurious hotels as well as a wide range of tourist lodgings have been built to accommodate the large numbers of visitors.

Of archaeological interest is the area called Kastri (Castle), where the remains of a settlement and cemetery have been found dating from before the arrival of the Parians.

Potos, a picturesque settlement.

Theologos

The history of Theologos begins in early times with its roots in that vague land somewhere between legend and distant fact, with tradition accompanying its history from the very beginning. Theologos was built with melancholy dignity, in Spartan surroundings in the middle of Thasos. The abundant clean water, the dense greenery, and remote location of the village was the reason why monks from Mount Athos came here and settled. They took advantage of these natural features, particularly the gushing springs, to build mills and monastery dependencies.

The founding of the first settlement of Theologos is associated with Turks settling in Thasos' two main villages. In the age when Thasos was beginning to fall into decline and become isolated from the outside world due to piracy, Theologos began developing into the most important village on the island. It played a leading part in the administration until the mid-19th century and assumed the management of the island's civil affairs as its capital. After liberation from the Turks, Theologos lost some of its old glory, but remains one of the largest villages on the island.

Theologos, a historic village in the centre of Thasos.

Useful Information

The lovely green island of Thasos, apart from being a place with a fascinating history and rare natural beauty, can also offer visitors everything they need for a perfect and truly unforgettable stay. Your days can be rich with any number of interesting activities, and whether you are of an athletic bent, a nature lover, a keen swimmer or looking for some lively night-life, there's an endless choice of things to do and places to see.

There are plenty of luxurious hotels and less expensive and bungalows on the island, built on the most beautiful spots either by the sea or higher up, but always surrounded by green trees and vegetation. The large numbers of visitors, especially in the summer months, can find a wide variety of accommodation.

This includes rooms to rent, and sometimes the ordinary residents of Thasos will offer to rent rooms in their own homes. Hospitality is, after all, one of the main traits of the people of Thasos, which is why, at the beginning of every new season, all of Thassos prepares to welcome the visitors to its shores.

One can get to the island by hydrofoil, by ferry, or in one of the private pleasure craft that cruise its beautiful picturesque bays. Getting to know Thasos is a truly special "journey" through its illustrious past up to the modern age.

In the pages that follow you will find all the information you need to know about camping, sports, shopping, entertainment, and short excursions on the island.

Camping

Thasos is ideal for camping. It has the most suitable locations in the shade of its wooded slopes and next to the deep blue sea. The beaches are inviting and many of them are in sheltered coves protected from all kinds of weather conditions. All the locations are beautiful which is why a large proportion of visitors to Thasos choose to go camping.

Sports

Swimming

The crystalline waters of the Aegean make swimming on Thasos a real pleasure. For those who seek the perfect beaches there is a tremendous variety, from rocky and wild with crashing waves, to sandy and shallow, or deep and pebbled. There are also little coves with hidden beaches that can you can only get to either by boat or by swimming to them. Swimming on Thasos is both a pleasure and an adventure.

Water-skiing

A good many visitors to Thasos enjoy water-skiing. Boats and equipment can be found on some of the island's better-known beaches.

Windsurfing

Windsurfs can be rented by the hour in all the most popular beaches. The waves on Paradisos beach are ideal for aficionados of this sport, but there are also other suitable beaches one can discover by exploring the island. Those who wish to compete can enter one of the privately-organised small-scale contests.

Sailing

Weather conditions in the area favour sailing, which is well established on the island. Sailing boats of various sizes are available for rent and are ideal for a trip round the island by sea.

Jet-ski - Banana - Parachute

For those who prefer something more adventurous and daring, jet-skis, bananas and parachutes can be rented at almost all the organised facilities at beaches and campsites.

Scuba-diving

Scuba-diving, spear-fishing, snorkelling or simply exploring the underwater depths is widespread on Thasos. Large numbers of spear-gun fishermen and scuba-divers roam the seas of Thasos every year.

Tennis

Tennis courts are usually available at camp-sites and larger hotel complexes.

Shopping

Attractive shopping facilities on Thasos are provided by quaint little shops and old established stores. Pedlars, from whom one can buy anything from a pin to a whole carpet, are on the streets everywhere.

The fine Thasian hand-weavings provide an outstanding combination of patterns and colours. There are also shops with pottery and statuettes representing events and people from antiquity in Thasos. Of special interest are the luxury jewellery shops with their stunning original jewellery and silver revetted icons. As for clothing and footwear, one can find some of the best-known brand names. Small shops and boutiques are scattered everywhere, but there are also kiosks along the roadsides which sell Thasian products including the popular spoon sweet called karydaki *(walnuts preserved in syrup), tasty olives and fine olive-oil.*

Food and Entertainment

One of the things that distinguishes Thasos is its good food. In addition to the fresh fish and seafood caught by local fishermen in the clean waters of the Aegean, there are also tavernas that feature grilled meat and fish, serving up veritable feasts every day.

Nestled between the fish tavernas on the seafront are small picturesque ouzeri *that serve delicious appetizers accompanied by ouzo. These little shops are the favourite haunts of fishermen and seamen, where one can hear the most amazing stories while enjoying a carafe of ouzo and some fresh sardines. In the mountains one can find tavernas specialising in grilled meat and fish, each one made with their own special recipes. What is truly unforgettable for visitors is the excellent wine, which they themselves have often helped to produce at the grape-crushing season.*

All over the island there are pastry shops serving an array of tempting sweets, pizza parlours, souvlaki shops, and picturesque ice-cream parlours, while for the more romantic, Thasos is full of restaurants and little tavernas in beautiful locations where the greenery blends in with the sea and the starry sky.

Many of the restaurants have live music and the dancing lasts until dawn. The nightlife on Thasos offers all the distractions one could ask for after a lazy day at the beach. In the evening, all parts of the island, roads, beaches, and night clubs are flooded with people, especially at Limenas, Limenaria, and Potos. All this activity makes strolls in the evening or even late at night an interesting experience. The numerous night clubs provide traditional music, songs and dances especially designed for visitors. There are bars and clubs everywhere, but most people gather at the small bars on the sea-front, where the entertainment goes on until dawn. Another customary phenomenon on Thasos are the small impromptu private beach parties where the fun can also last until the wee hours.

Bibliography

Lazaridis, D. «Η Θάσος», *Thessaloniki, 1958*

Vakalopoulos A. «Η ιστορία της Θάσου, 1453-1912» *Thessaloniki, 1984*

French Archaelogical School «Οδηγός της Θάσου» *Athens, 1974*

Sotireli Ch. «Ιστορία της Θάσου και τουριστικός οδηγός της νήσου» *Kavala, 1967*

Thasian Association of Kavala «Θασιακά» *magazine in Greek, Vols I-X*